Conventions used:

Keyboard:
Keys to be pressed are enclosed in parenthesis such as: press (Enter).

Text to be typed, when included in an exercise step will be shaded. For example:
Type *No Fault Travel* and then press (Enter).

Mouse Operations:

Click: refers to clicking the left mouse button

Right-click: refers to clicking the right mouse button

Drag: refers to holding the left mouse button down and moving the mouse

Be sure to visit out our website: www.Pro-aut.com to order these workbooks in quantity.

Published by:

Pro-Aut Training and Consulting, Inc.
1024 Hemlock Ave.
Lewiston, ID 83501

You can also visit: www.LutherMaddy.com to contact the author, or see other resources available for this workbook.

Table of Contents

Welcome to Word 2016 Basics

This series of workbook/reference manuals is designed to get you working more productively with MS Word. You may be using this book on your own or in a class. Either way, this module will focus on the basics; the things every Word user should know to use Word to the fullest. In addition to learning basic Word features, you'll begin to learn more about using it more productively.

The difference between simply using Word and using it for the utmost productivity is huge. I encourage you to spend some time going over the topics covered in this module, even if you've been using Word for quite a while. Invariably, there will be some things you'll learn that will make you a better, more productive user.

This workbook is meant to be used in its entirety. Lessons build on the files created in previous lessons. Start at Lesson #1 and work through the lessons in order. Even if you are familiar with some of the concepts presented in the early lessons, you will likely learn more efficient ways to execute those features. Your existing skills will enable you to complete them very quickly. And, who knows, you may even learn a thing or two in those lessons as well.

Luther M. Maddy IIII, Ph.D.

Lesson #1: Creating and Saving Documents

In this lesson you will learn to:

Create Documents
Save Documents
Modify the Status Bar Display
Change the View
Use the Print Preview Feature

Lesson #1: Creating and Saving Documents

The Word Window

1.   Start Word if needed.

You can start Word several ways. Depending on your version of Windows, you may have to find it among the list of applications on your computers, or you may have an icon to start it on your Desktop.

When you first open Word it will display its start screen. Here you can open a document you have recently worked on, or start a new one using one of several predefined themes or with a blank page.

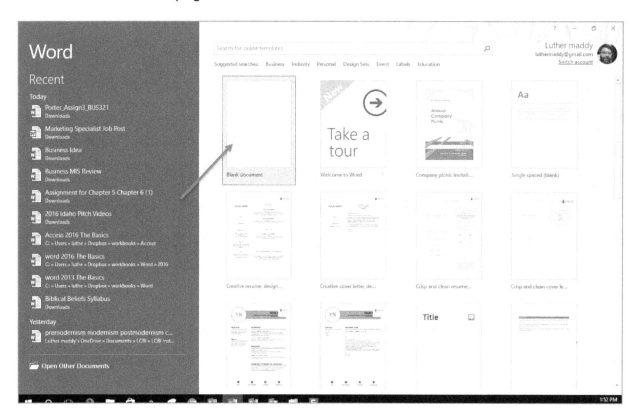

2.   Click the Blank document thumbnail.

To learn to create your own documents in Word, you'll start with a blank document which is Word's equivalent to a blank sheet of paper.

You should see a blinking vertical bar which is called the insertion point. The insertion point is commonly referred to as the cursor. Any text you type will appear at that location. The insertion point also shows you which text will be erased or changed if you are editing.

Take a few minutes to examine the Word window. Then examine the illustration on the next page for more information about what you are seeing in the Word window.

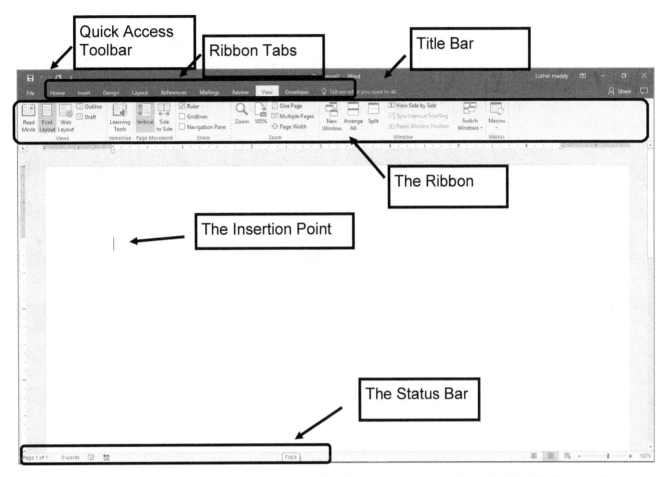

The Title Bar: Identifies the program or application you are working in. It will display the name of the document you are working on. After you created and Save a document, that name you give that document will appear on the title bar.

The Ribbon: The Ribbon gives you quick access to the feature you are working on. You can display different commands by clicking the Tabs above the ribbon. The ribbon will change, depending on what features you are working within Word.

The Quick Access toolbar: Provides a quick way to access commonly used commands, like saving a document, or undoing your last action.

The Status Bar: The Status Bar appears at the very bottom of the Word window and keeps you informed as to which page you are working on. You can modify the status bar display to show you many things about your document. You will learn about this later in this lesson.

The Insertion point or Cursor: The insertion point lets you know where you are on the screen for text editing. As you type, letters will appear at the insertion point's location.

3.   In an empty Word document window, type the following, ensuring that you press the (Enter) key only at the end of each paragraph.

MS Word is a very powerful word processing program. With it, you can easily create and format your documents. You can also easily perform tasks that were once very complex such as envelopes, labels and forms.

As you learn more about MS Word, you will come to appreciate its power and ease of use. Just remember that learning any new program takes time. Just be patient and you will soon be creating documents like a professional word processor.

Remember that the shading in the above paragraphs in just showing you that you will type this text. You will see that throughout this manual when you are to type. You don't need to shade the text you type in your documents, unless specifically told to do so.

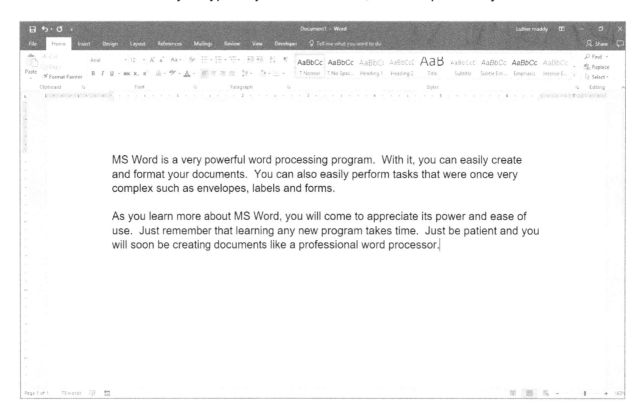

Depending on the default (automatic) line and paragraph settings in Word, you may automatically get a blank line between your first and second paragraph. If you do not and want to have a line between the two, you can create the blank line between these two paragraphs by pressing (Enter) a second time after the first paragraph.

Your screen may not look exactly like the illustration, depending on the view you have selected. We'll discuss view settings in the next couple of pages. The blank areas around the text in the illustration are the document margins.

Saving Documents

If you do not want to lose everything you have typed, you will need to save the Word document. Currently this document is stored in your computer's RAM (Random Access Memory). When you lose power, or turn off your computer, everything in RAM is lost. Saving stores the file on a hard drive, flash drive or cloud storage.

Once saved, you can then retrieve (Open) it again when you need it at a later date. You should develop the habit of saving frequently. If you do not, you may have to re-type some long portions of text. Since hard drives can also crash, it is a good idea to store important documents in at least two places to ensure against their loss. For example, you can store the novel you are creating on your computer's hard drive and also on a flash (thumb) drive or on a cloud drive such as Microsoft's OneDrive. This way, should one copy of your file be lost, you have another copy.

To save a document for the first and subsequent times, use the Save command.

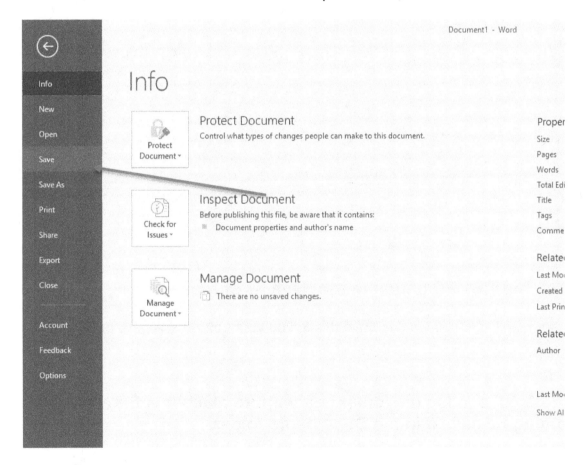

4. Click File on the Ribbon and then choose Save.

You could also access the Save command from the Quick Access toolbar which is located above the File menu option.

The Save As Screen

When you choose the Save command for the first time, Word will display the Save As screen. This is because you have not yet saved this file and Word needs you to specify where you want to save this file and the name you want to give the file. You will refer to the file by is name when you want to retrieve it later.

Before actually saving, it is a good idea to notice the drive and folder where you are placing this file. This makes locating the file much easier. There are likely many folders on the hard drive and you may even have several drives available where you can save it. Knowing where to look for a file makes finding it easier and faster.

While there are many locations available for you to save this document, we'll assume you are saving it in the Documents folder (or library) on your local hard drive.

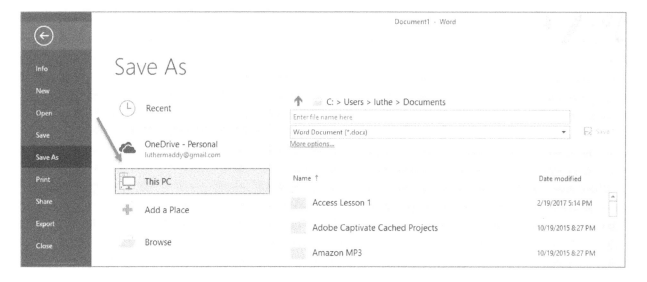

5.   Click the This PC option in the Save As screen.

You are informing Word you want to save this file on your computer's hard drive and in the Documents folder.

6.   If desired, choose the folder you want to place this file, or do nothing to leave it in the Documents folder.

Where you save your file really does not matter as long as you remember where you stored it. You may choose another folder or be instructed to do so and that will be all right. For this book's purposes, we'll assume you have used the Documents folder.

The next step is to name this file. When you name a file, you want to give it a name that is descriptive so you can recall the file's contents in a large list of files. Filenames can be up to 255 characters in length, but file names of this size can be quite unwieldy. Spaces are allowed in filenames, but you should avoid using punctuation or other symbols because some of these are not allowed in file names.

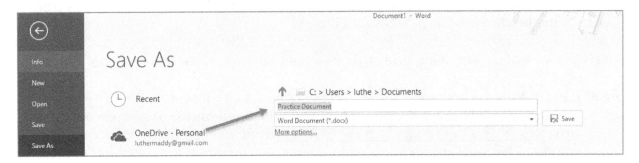

7.   Type *Practice Document* in the File Name textbox and click Save to save the file.

Save vs. Save As

You selected the Save command but Word displayed the Save As dialog box. This is because you have not already named this file. As you modify a document, you will want to save often. However, when you do, choose the Save command, not the Save As command. When you choose Save, Word will overwrite the previous version with the newest version and use the same name.

If you complete saving an existing document with the Save As command Word will ask if you want to replace the existing file with the one you are saving. If you are working on the same document, you will, of course, want to replace the old with the new. Using the Save command eliminates this extra, sometimes confusing question that Word asks.

One purpose of using the Save As command is to make a copy of a file with a different name or in a different location for backup purposes. When you choose Save, Word automatically keeps the same name and the same location. Using the Save As command allows you to change the location, name, or both. If you do change either of these, you then have two files, either in the same location with two different names or perhaps with the same name but at two different locations or drives.

Changing Views

Word has several views you can use as you edit and scroll through your document. The two most commonly used are Draft and Print Layout. Of the two, the Print Layout view is usually preferred as it lets you see your document as looks printed. You can change the view using the View tab or the View buttons on the right of the Status Bar. Some of the views available in MS Word are:

Draft View: Not all formatting and other page features will show in this mode.

Print Layout View: This mode shows the document as it will when printed. Print Layout also displays both the vertical and horizontal rulers. It also shows the top margin. This is very close to a WYSIWYG (what you see is what you get) editing mode. This view will show many formatting options that do not appear in Draft, such as Headers and Footers.

Read Mode: This mode optimizes the view for reading a document on a computer screen. This mode, by default shows two pages side by side. It also gives you the option of seeing the document just as it would appear if printed.

You will now try changing the view of the Word document you just created.

1.   Click the View tab above the ribbon. If the Ruler option is not on, turn it on then click the Draft tool on the Ribbon.

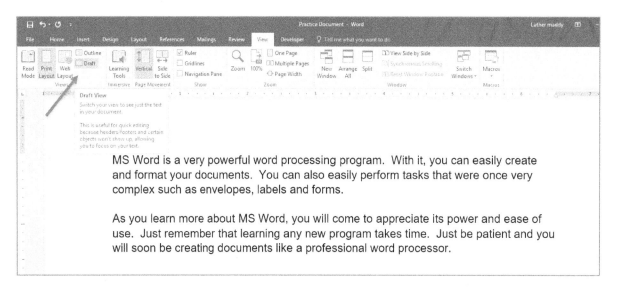

Notice the ruler along the left side of the window is not visible. You may also notice there is no empty space at the top of the page.

2.   Now, click the Print Layout tool on the Ribbon.

The vertical ruler is now visible. This is usually the preferred view when creating and editing documents in Word.

To change views you can also use the View shortcuts on the right side of the Status Bar or use keyboard shortcuts. There is no right or wrong way to switch views or select any other command in MS Word. There is usually more than one way to select Word commands.

Zoom Settings

In addition to changing the view settings, Word also allows you to choose from pre-defined or custom zoom settings. These settings include allowing you to increase the size of the text for editing purposes or shrink the view so you are looking at an entire page. You can access the zoom settings on the View tab.

1.   Display the View tab.

You should now see the View ribbon options including the option of toggling the Ruler on and off.

2.   Click One Page in the Zoom group on the Ribbon.

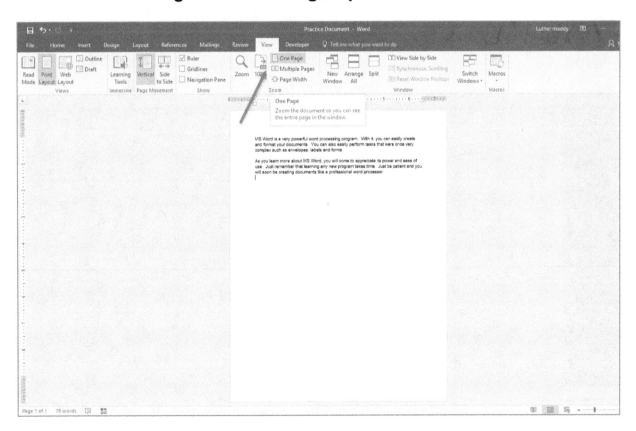

You should now see an entire page of this document. This setting is very useful when you are moving and copying pictures and paragraphs on the same page.

3.   Click Page Width tool in the Zoom group on the Ribbon.

This setting spreads the text out to fill the width of your screen.

4.   Click 100% in the Zoom group on the Ribbon.

This is the normal or default setting in Word.

5.   Choose the View option you prefer, 100% or Page Width.

Many of the screen shots in this text will use the Page Width setting. This allows the text to be more visible in this workbook.

Print Preview

The only true WYSIWYG (what you see is what you get) mode is the Print Preview mode. Here you see the document exactly as it will print.

1.   Click the File menu and then choose Print.

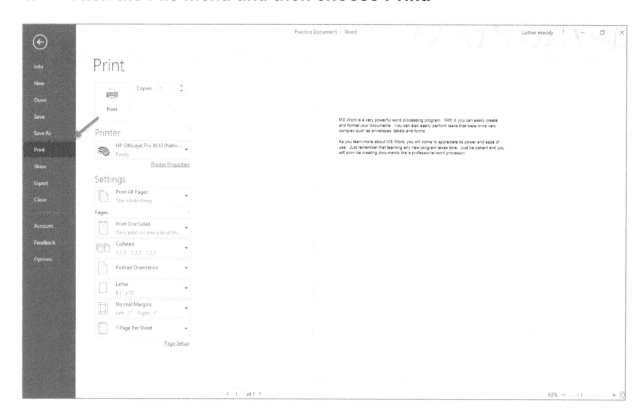

Word will now display the Print menu, which includes a preview of this document.

Printing Documents

The Print menu allows you to choose several options for printing the document. The *Printer* section includes a drop down menu where you can select a printer, if more than one printer is available.

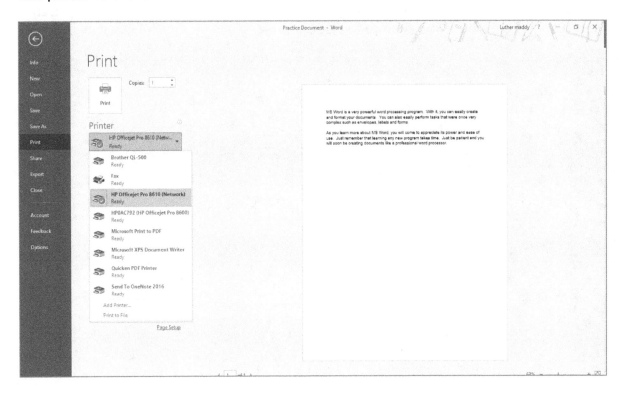

The Printer Properties link below the selected printer allows you to choose printer specific options such as, changing the print quality, printing in black and white if you have a color printer and other options tied directly to your printer.

The *Settings* section allows you to specify options such as; duplexing (double sided printing) if your printer has the capability, specific pages to print or paper size and orientation.

To save paper, you do not need to actually print this document in this lesson.

Closing a Document:

Closing a document allows you to "put it away" and work on something else. As long as you have saved your document after making changes none of those changes will be lost. If you have made changes and have not previously saved, Word will warn you to save the document when you attempt to close the file.

2.   **Click the Close command in the File menu to close this document.**

Lesson #1: Skill Builder

After closing the document you were working on, you now need to inform Word that you would like to create another document.

1. From the File menu click the New option.

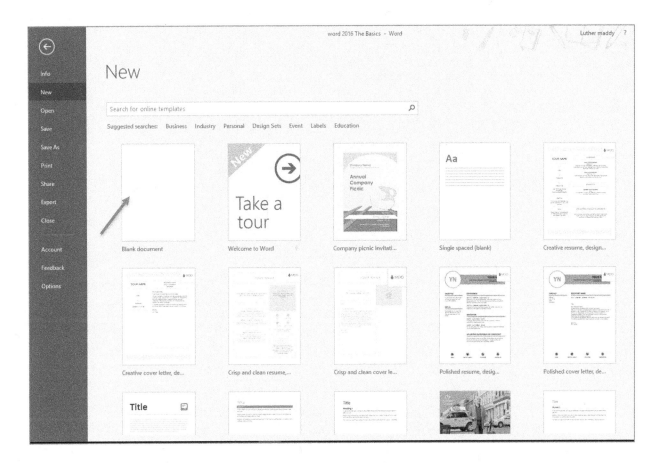

2. Click the Blank Document thumbnail to create another new, blank document.

3. Type the following text:

As requested, we are sending you a list of the current airfares from Boise to Maui. Please be advised that these fares could change at any moment. If you're interested at all, let us know as soon as possible.

Sincerely,

Maria Byrd
Booking Agent

4.   Save this file as *Airfare Request* and close the document.

To make this file easier to find, you should probably save this document in the same folder you used for the Practice Document.

Lesson #2: Basic Editing

In this lesson you will learn to:

Open Documents
Preview Documents
Move the Insertion Point
Delete Existing Text using the Keyboard
Change Spelling and Grammar Check Settings
Save Existing Documents

Lesson #2: Basic Editing

Opening Files

Once you have closed a document, you will need to open it before you can continue working with the file. To open a previously saved document you will use the Open command on the File menu.

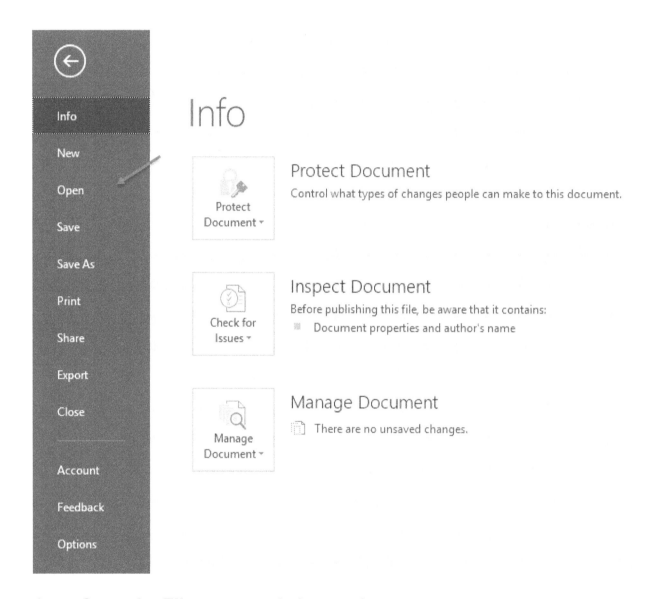

1.   Open the File menu and choose Open.

The Open screen provides a list of files you have most recently worked with. The Practice Document should appear near the top of this list. To open this file you can simply click on it. To open a file that is not one you have accessed recently, you will need to access the drive or other storage location you stored the file in earlier. After selecting the storage location, then navigate to the folder where you saved the file to locate it.

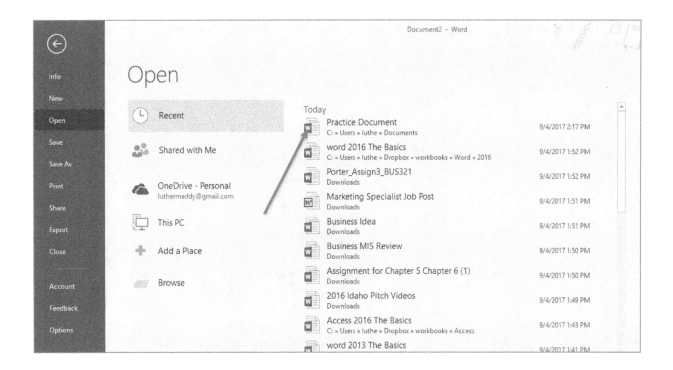

2.   In the list of recently accessed files, click once on *Practice Document* to select and open the file.

Moving the Insertion Point

The insertion point, sometimes called the cursor, shows you precisely where you are in the text. When you begin typing, the new text will appear at the insertion point's location. The insertion point's location is also very important when editing, adding or deleting text.

You can move the insertion point with the mouse by simply clicking where you want the insertion point. You can also move the insertion point using the keyboard. When moving around in a large document, the keyboard is often faster than attempting to use the mouse.

The power of the Control (Ctrl) key

As you examine the abridged list of keyboard shortcuts to move the insertion point and delete text you should notice there are two combinations. First is the single key, such as the (End) key. Pressing the single key will move the insertion point or delete some text. However, when you press and hold the (Control) key before pressing the single more or deletion key, Word will either move farther or delete more. It's a simple concept that is used with many movement and deletion keyboard shortcut keystrokes.

Here are some of the keyboard commands that you can use to move the insertion point within your document:

Move to:	Keystrokes
Beginning of Line	(Home)
End of Line	(End)
Top of Document	(Control+Home)
End of Document	(Control+End)
Up one line	(Up Arrow)
Down one line	(Down Arrow)
Up one paragraph	(Control+Up Arrow)
Down one paragraph	(Control+Down Arrow)
Top of previous page	(Control+Page Up)
Top of next page	(Control+Down Arrow)
One character right	(Right Arrow)
One character left	(Left Arrow)
One word right	(Control+Right Arrow)
One word left	(Control+Left Arrow)

Delete Existing Text with the Keyboard

Erase character right of Insertion point	(Delete)
Erase character left of Insertion point	(Backspace)
Erase word left of insertion point	(Control+Backspace)*
Erase word right of insertion point	(Control+Delete)*

Insertion point should be at the beginning of a word

In this portion of Lesson #2 you will use the keyboard to move the insertion point and then edit the text in the Practice document.

1.   After opening the Practice Document, press (Control+Down Arrow) until you are at the beginning of the second paragraph.

When opening a document, Word automatically places the insertion point at the top of the document. (Control+Down Arrow) moves the insertion point down one paragraph each time you press it. If you created a blank line between these two paragraphs by pressing the (Enter) key, Word considers the blank line a paragraph.

Whenever you use the Control, Shift or Alt keys, you must keep that key held down while you press the other key to use keyboard shortcuts.

2. **Press (Control+Right Arrow) twice to move to the beginning of the word *learn*.**

3. **Press (Control+Delete) to delete this word.**
This deletes the word to the right of the insertion point.

4. **Type the word *gain* and press (space) to replace the deleted word.**

5. **Press (Control+Right Arrow) twice again to move to the beginning of *MS Word* in this sentence.**

6. **Press (Control+Backspace) to delete the word *about*, the word left of the insertion point.**

7. **Type *experience with* and press (space).**

You have replaced the deleted word and your text should appear as that below.

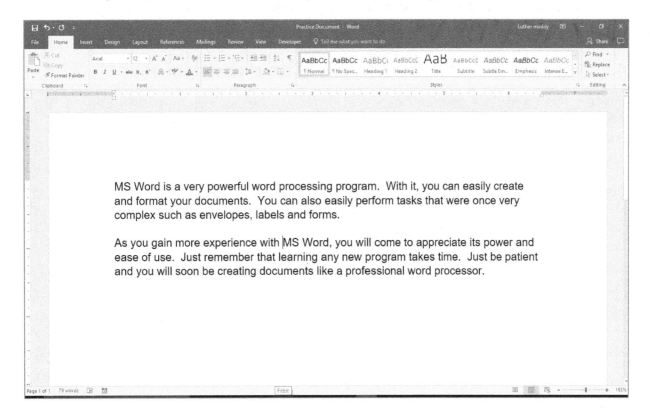

Auto Spell Check

Word automatically checks your spelling and grammar as you type. Word will underline in red misspelled words or words not in its dictionary. When it finds a possible grammatical or typographical error, Word will underline the possible error in blue.

To quickly correct a word that is underlined in red, move the mouse pointer into that word and right-click. When you do, you will see a list of possible spelling suggestions. If the correct spelling is there, just click it and Word will make the correction for you. If Word underlines words that are spelled correctly, you can select Add from the Spelling shortcut menu to permanently add the word to the spell check dictionary.

You can also use the mouse to move the insertion point.

1.   **Use the mouse and click inside the word** *processing* **in the first line of the first paragraph.**

2.   **Now, delete the letter "*o*" in this word and replace it with the letter "*e*".**

3.   **Move outside this word and you will see that Word has underlined the word** *precessing* **in red.**

4.   **Move the mouse pointer into this word and right-click.**

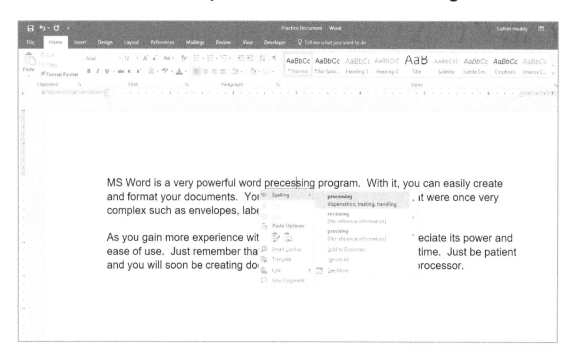

5.   **From the list of suggestions, click** *processing* **to correct this error.**

Adjusting the Grammar Check Settings

When Word is first installed the default (automatic) grammar check settings are very basic. If you know you have a specific recurring problem with grammar, you may find that Word does not flag those errors. Leaving critical grammar errors in your document is not very desirable, and could be very embarrassing. To help prevent that, Word will let you adjust the errors it looks for and flags in your documents.

In this portion of this lesson you will adjust the grammar check settings to look for errors Word currently ignores in your documents. You can adjust the grammar check settings and many other default settings in the Word Options dialog box. You access the Word Options dialog box from the File menu.

1.   **In the first line of text move to the beginning of the word *is*. Then, press (Delete) until the word is deleted.**

2.   **Now, type *are* in place of the word is you just deleted.**

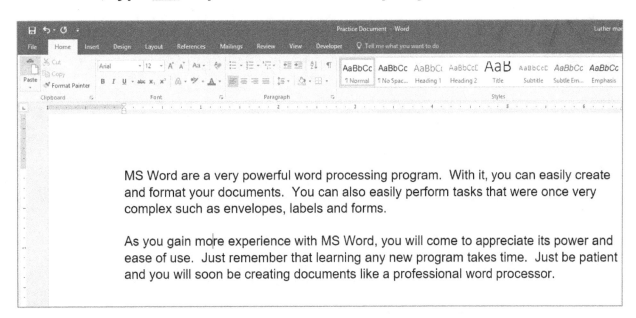

Notice that Word does not alert you to the error you just created in your document. If you had difficulty recognizing subject/verb agreement errors, leaving this error in your document could be embarrassing.

You will now adjust Word's grammar settings so that it will look for and highlight errors in subject/verb agreement.

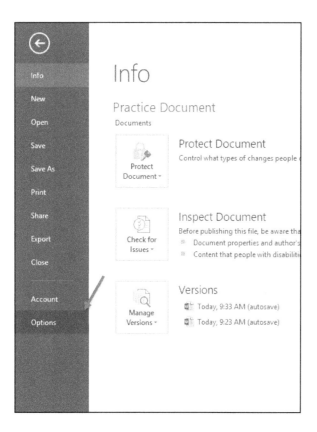

3. Click File to open the File menu and then choose Options.

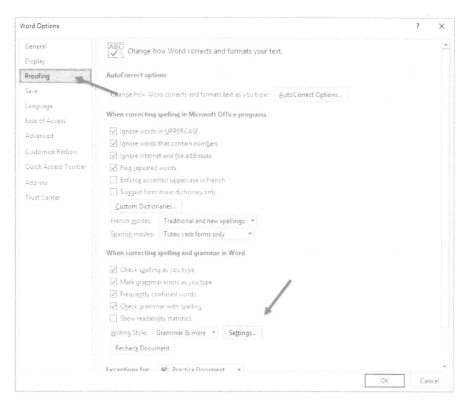

You should now see the Word Options dialog box. Here you can adjust many of Word's default settings.

4.   **In the Word Options dialog box, select Proofing and then click the Settings... button in the "When correcting spelling and grammar in Word" section.**

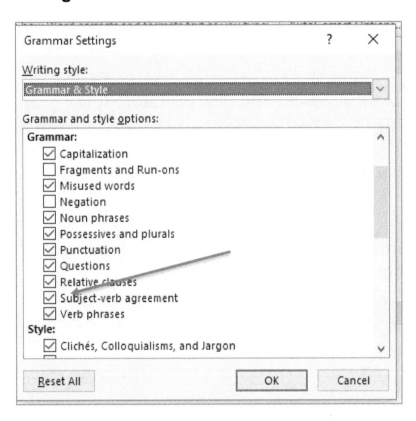

You should now see the Grammar Settings dialog box. Here you can specify what grammar errors you want Word to check. For this exercise, you will turn on Subject-verb agreement checking.

5.   **In the Grammar Settings dialog box, scroll down until you find the Subject-verb agreement option. Turn this option on and click OK.**

6.   **Click OK again to leave the Word Options dialog box and return to the document.**

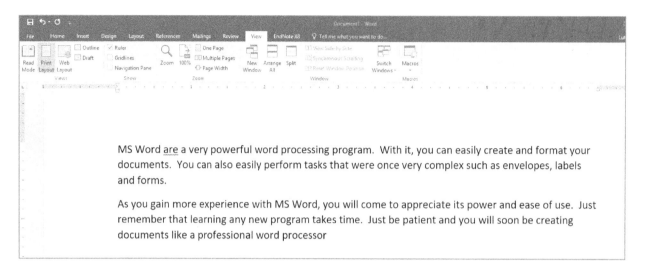

You should notice that Word has found the error and alerted you.

7. **Right-click in the word *are* underlined in blue, and then select *is* in the correction options to correct this error.**

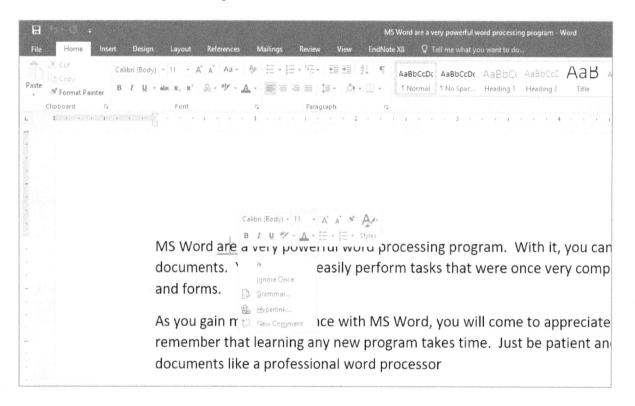

Saving an Existing Document

When you save a document that you have already saved, you can choose the Save rather than the Save As command. When you choose Save, Word will save the document with the name it already has. This makes the process of saving frequently very easy.

8.   Click the File menu and choose Save.

You may want to try this operation by clicking the Save tool on the Quick Access toolbar.

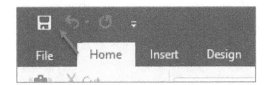

You can also try the keyboard shortcut (Control+S) to save the open document.

When you execute the Save command, Word saved the file as it is right now. The changes you made are saved, and you will not lose them. You will want to develop the habit of regularly saving your document as you work on it. This will ensure that you do not lose any important work.

9.   Click the File menu and choose Close

The document is now closed. Now you must either create a new document or open an existing document.

Lesson #2: Skill Builder

1.   Open the file named *Airfare Request*.

2.   Using the features covered in Lesson #2, make changes illustrated below. Delete the text that has a line through it and add the text that appears in bold.

As requested, we are ~~sending~~ **enclosing** ~~you~~ a list of the current airfares from Boise to Maui. Please be advised that these fares ~~could~~ **are subject to** change at any moment. ~~If you're interested at all, let~~ **Let** us know as soon as possible **when you're ready to book one of these flights**.

Sincerely,

Maria Byrd
Booking Agent

When done with this skill builder your document should appear as that below:

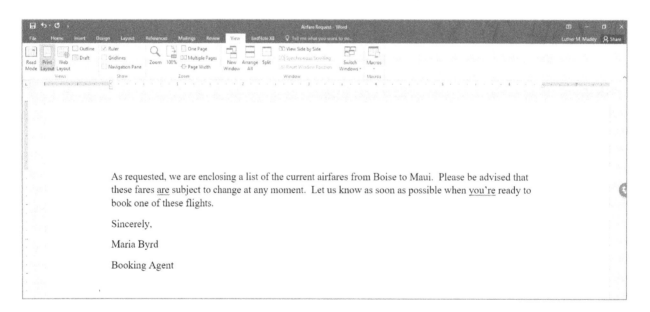

Note: Your lines may break differently than the illustration depending on the font and type size you are currently using. You can just ignore that for now. You'll learn to change fonts and sizes in an upcoming lesson.

Word may have flagged some potential grammar errors. You can ignore those for now.

3.   Save this file with the same name (File, Save) then Close it.

Lesson #3: Selecting, Moving, Copying and Enhancing

In this lesson you will learn to:

Select Text with Mouse and Keyboard
Cut, Copy and Paste Text
Drag and Drop Text
Use the Undo Command
Enhance Existing Text
Enhance New Text

Lesson #3: Selecting, Moving, Copying, and Enhancing text

Selecting Text

To change the appearance of existing text or move or copy text, you must first select it. Selected text will appear with a gray background, and selecting is sometimes called highlighting text. But, highlighting text is actually a different command, so we'll keep calling it selecting text in this workbook.

You can select text using the keyboard or the mouse. One very simple way to select text is to simply click and drag across it. However, when you want to select large portions of text this method becomes impractical, so here are some other methods you can use to select text.

Selecting text with the mouse within text

Select irregular text portions   Click and drag

You can also position the insertion point at the beginning of the text you want to select and then move the mouse pointer to the end of the text you want to select. To finish the process hold the (Shift) key and click. The text between the insertion point and where the mouse pointer was located should be selected when you click the mouse with the (Shift) key held down.

Text to Select	Method with the mouse
Select One Word	Double Click on that word
Select One Paragraph	Triple Click in that paragraph
Select One Sentence	Press (Control) and click in that sentence
Select a Column	Press and hold the (Alt) and drag

Using the Selection area (left margin) and the mouse

The selection area is the left margin, outside of the actual text. You can see the selection area when you are the Print Layout view. When you move mouse pointer into the selection area it will become an arrow rather than an I-beam.

Text to Select	Selection area method
Select One Line	Click in the selection area to the left of the line
Select One Paragraph	Double click to the left of the paragraph
Select the Entire Document	Triple click in the selection area

Using the keyboard

Text to Select	Keyboard Method
Select One Paragraph	Move to the beginning of the paragraph then (Shift)+(Control)+Down).
Select to End of Document	Move to beginning of desired text, (Shift)+(Control)+(End)
Select Entire Document	(Control)+(A)

Selecting Non-Contiguous Text
Sometimes you may want to select portions of your document that are in different areas (non-contiguous). To do this, select the first portion of text, then hold the (Control) key and select the other portion of text. This is useful when you want to enhance (bold, underline, etc..) multiple portions of your document that do not occur together.

Moving (Cutting) and Copying text

To move cut or copy text you can:
   a. Select the text you want to move
   b. Choose Cut (to move) or Copy
   c. Move the insertion point where you want the moved or copied text to be
   d. Choose Paste

What can make this process confusing is that you can choose the Cut, Copy, and Paste commands several ways. You can find these commands in the Clipboard group on the Home tab, or you can use Shortcut keys. You can also access these commands with shortcut menus (right-click). This lesson will give you an idea of the variety available with these commands.

You will now open the document you created and move and copy portions of the text. You will also change the appearance of existing text by selecting that text and making the desired format changes.

1. Open Practice Document.

2. Move the mouse pointer into the text of the first paragraph and click three times to select the entire paragraph.

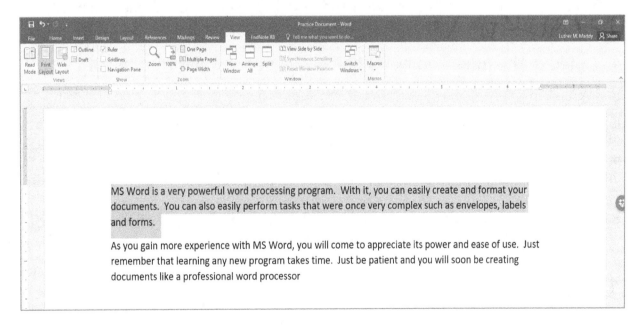

If you're unable to select the text by triple-clicking, make sure you hold the mouse still while you click. The gray highlighting shows you the text is selected.

3. With this paragraph selected, click the Cut (scissors) tool on the Ribbon.

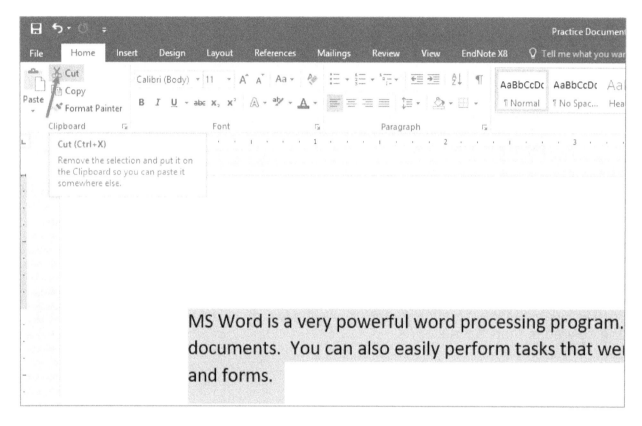

The paragraph you selected will now disappear. The paragraph is not gone forever. It is being stored in the Windows clipboard. The next step is to move the insertion point where you want the paragraph to be moved and then choose Paste.

4. Move the insertion point below the second paragraph with (Control+End).

If you cannot get the insertion point below the paragraph, you neglected to press (Enter) at the end of the second paragraph when creating this document. To correct this, just press (Enter) at the end of the second paragraph now to end this paragraph. If the insertion point **did** move below the second paragraph, you do not need to press (Enter).

5. After moving the insertion point, click the Paste (clipboard) tool on the Ribbon.

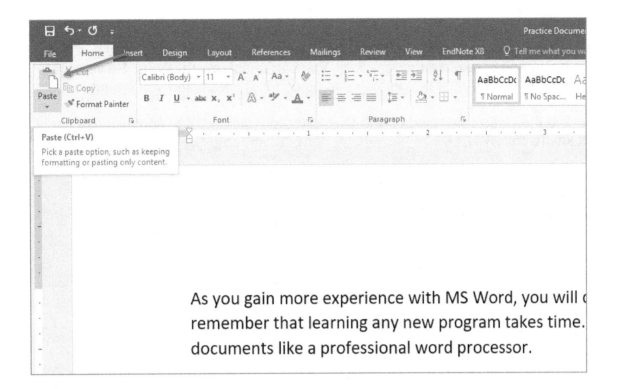

The Paste Options Smart Tag

The paragraph that was at the top of the document originally should now be moved below what was the second paragraph.

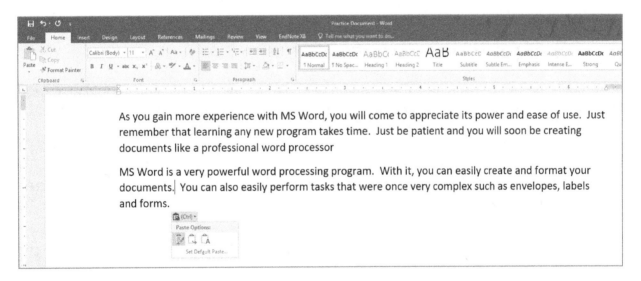

You may also notice an icon appears at the bottom of the paragraph you just moved. This is a smart tag. Smart tags give you additional options after you perform certain commands.

Clicking the drop-down arrow of a smart tag key reveals the options available from that tag. This smart tag allows you to choose options that control the formatting of the pasted paragraph. Since this document has no additional formatting, we'll ignore this smart tag for now.

Using the Undo Command

Whenever you are not happy with the results of a change you just made, you can use the undo command to reverse that change. You can undo several times. However, be careful not to go too far back or you may end up undoing something you meant to keep.

You can find the Undo command on the Quick Access toolbar. You can also use the shortcut key (Control+Z).

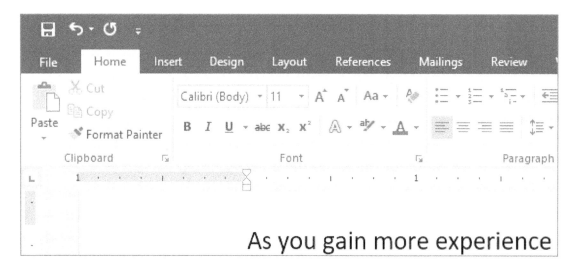

6.   **Click the Undo tool on the Quick Access Toolbar twice to undo the move of the first paragraph.**

Using the Shortcut Menu to Move and Copy

If you use the mouse to select the text you intend to move or copy, you should also use the mouse to select the move or copy commands. The most efficient way to use the mouse is to employ shortcut menus. Using Word's shortcut menus, you can quickly choose the commands you need.

1.   **If needed, select the top paragraph in this document (click three times).**

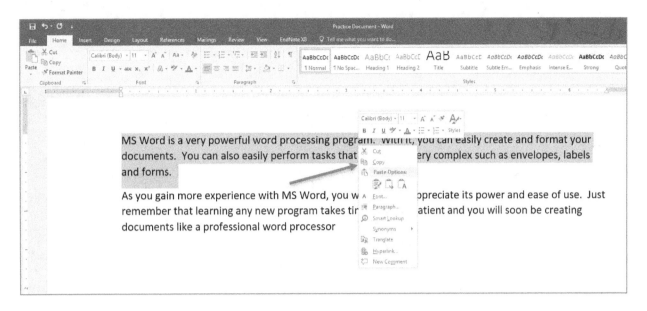

2. **Move the mouse pointer into the selected paragraph. Right-click to see the menu shown above.**

3. **From the shortcut menu, click Copy.**

4. **Now, move the mouse pointer below the second paragraph and right-click.**

   If you cannot get below the last paragraph you need to press (Enter) to create a blank line.

5. **From the shortcut menu, click the first icon, Keep Source Formatting in the Paste Options section.**

As you move into the Paste Options section of this shortcut menu, Word will display the copied text in the document to let you preview the result of each paste option. The copy is only completed after you click the icon in the Paste Options dialog box.

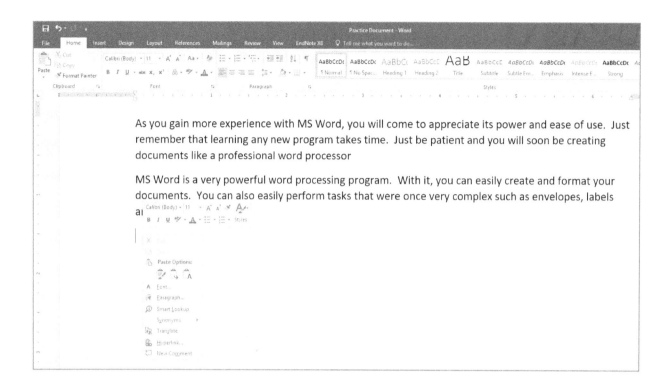

You have now copied the first paragraph using shortcut menus.

6. **Move to the beginning of the paragraph you just added with (Control+Up Arrow). If needed, insert a blank line above it by pressing (Enter).**

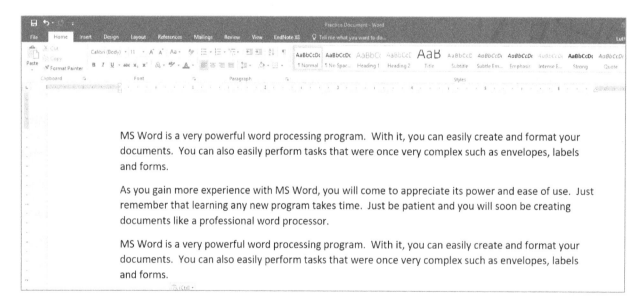

Your practice document should now appear like the example above.

Using Drag and Drop to Move and Copy

In addition to the Cut and Paste method, you can also drag selected text to move or copy. However, this method works best when the source and destination are on the same screen.

In other words, the drag and drop method does not work well when you are trying to move or copy text from one page to another because scrolling through a multiple page document is not very accurate. Aside from being inefficient, this practice can lead to confusion and messed up documents as portions of text do not end up where you intended to move or copy them.

To move or copy using the drag and drop method, you first select the text you want to move or copy. Then move the mouse pointer into this text. Next, press and hold the **Ctrl (Control key)** and drag to the destination. When you release the mouse button the text will be copied to that location.

1. **Select the second paragraph in this document (click three times).**

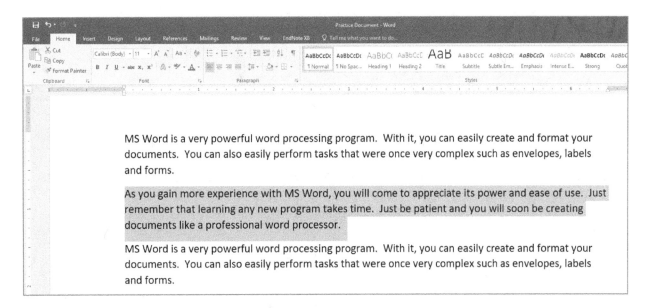

2. **Move the mouse pointer into this paragraph and press and hold (Ctrl).**

3. **Keeping the (Ctrl) key held down, move the mouse pointer to the bottom of this document and release the mouse button.**

4. **Press the (Down) arrow to deselect the paragraph.**

After moving or copying, it is very important to deselect the text. If you do not and begin typing, the text you just moved, or enhanced, will be replaced with the new text. Deselecting simply removes the gray highlighting and returns the text to the editing mode. You can deselect text by moving the insertion point somewhere else in the document.

5.   If needed, add a blank line above the paragraph you just copied by pressing (Enter) at the beginning of that paragraph.

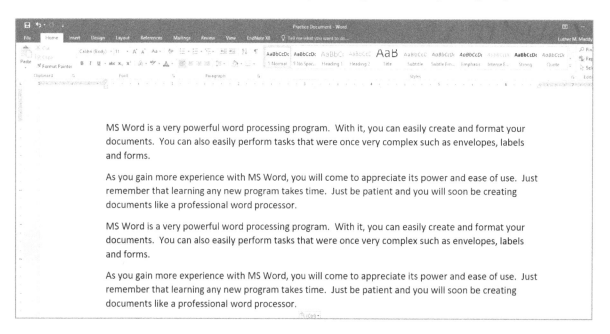

You document should now appear like the above.

You have explored several ways to move and copy. The best approach for now is the one you can remember. As you become more experienced with Word, you will learn that knowing more than one way to accomplish a task will increase your productivity.

Enhancing Existing Text

To change the appearance of text that is already created (existing text), you must first select the portion of the text you wish to change. Then simply apply the formatting options you want, such as Bold, Italic or other Font attributes.

1.   Press and hold (Ctrl) and click anywhere in the first sentence of the first paragraph.

(Control+click) selects an entire sentence. As with editing, the (Control) key adds functionality when selecting text.

2.   With this sentence selected, click the Bold tool in the Home tab on the Ribbon.

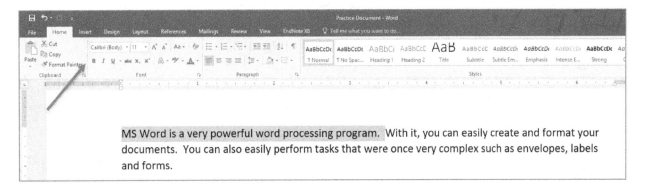

The first sentence in this document should now be boldfaced. Boldfacing text causes it to appear darker than the text around it. If you cannot see the Bold tool, click the Home tab.

3.   Select the second paragraph by triple clicking in it.

4.   In the Font group in the Home tab, click the Font dialog box launcher (the ⌐⌐ to the right of Font) to display the Font dialog box.

In this portion of the lesson you are using the Font dialog box to change the appearance of the text. You could also use the tools on the Ribbon to change these options. The Font dialog box however, allows you select some options that do not appear on the Ribbon.

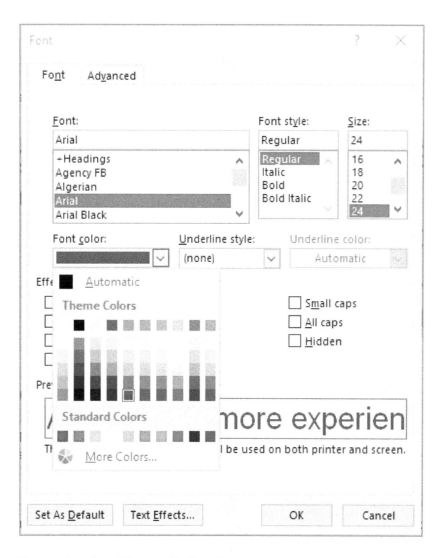

5.   In the Font dialog box, choose Arial from the font selections.

Scroll down the list of font faces to find Arial if necessary.

The Preview section will show you how the selected text will appear with the options chosen in the Font dialog box.

6.   Click in the Size section of this dialog box and select a font size of 24.

7.   Click the Font Color drop down list button. From the list of colors, click the Blue, Accent 1, Darker 50% option and then click OK.

Clicking the More Colors option in the color selection area provides many additional colors than shown listed on the main color selector.

You can try the More Colors option on your own as you are experimenting with Word. The best way to learn a software program is through experimenting on your own. This workbook guides you through many of Word's features, but you should not hesitate to practice the things you are learning here on your own.

If, when you return to your document, all the paragraphs became larger and Dark Blue, click the Undo tool on the Quick Access Toolbar or with the shortcut (Control+Z). When you do, only the second paragraph should be changed.

8. Deselect this paragraph by pressing (DOWN arrow).

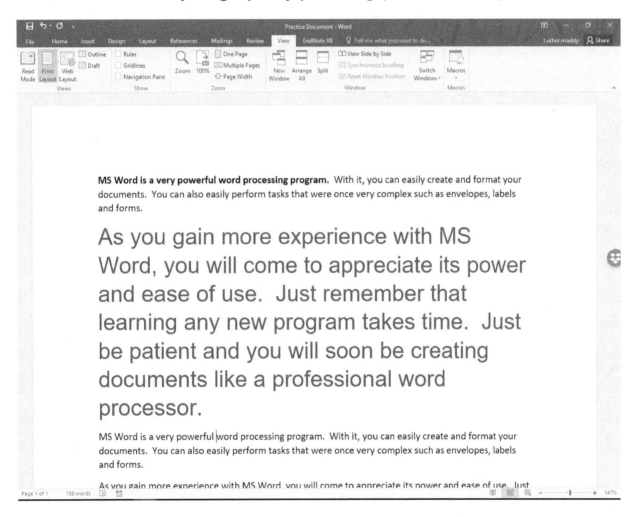

Your document similar to the image above.

Using the Format Painter

If you want another portion of text to be formatted in the same way as some other text in your document, you do not have to repeat all the formatting commands you used originally. Instead, you can use the Format Painter. The Format Painter will copy formatting from one portion of text and allow you to use that formatting on additional text. The Format Painter is located in the Clipboard group on the Home tab.

You will now see how the Format painter command works.

1.   Move the insertion point anywhere in the text that is formatted with the Blue, Large font and click the Format Painter tool on the Home tab.

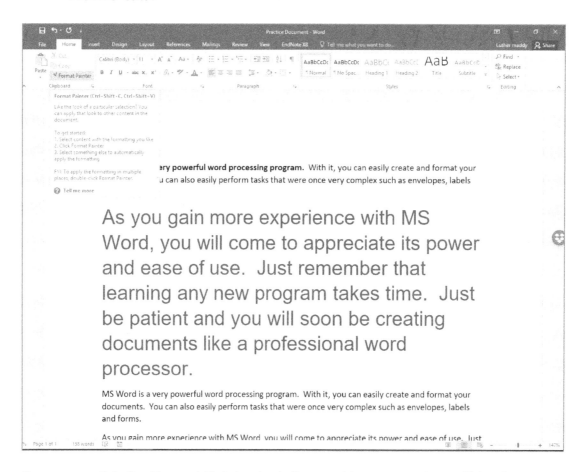

Once you click the Format Painter tool, the next text you select will be formatted just as the text was where you clicked this tool. Word will format only the next text you select. Double-clicking the Format Painter tool will cause all text you select until you click the Format Painter tool again to be reformatted.

2.   After clicking the Format Painter tool, move the mouse into the first paragraph and select the two consecutive words, *your documents*.

You can select these two words by clicking at the beginning, holding the mouse down and dragging to the end of the text. The text you just selected should now be formatted the same as the entire second paragraph.

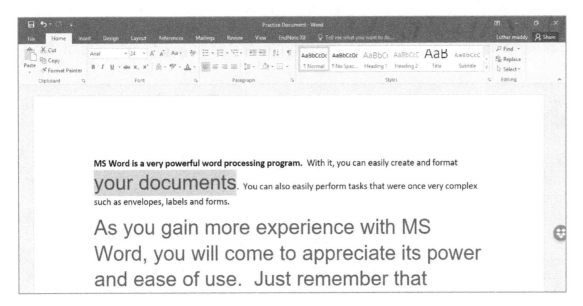

If you find more text changed than should have, use the Undo command to correct this.

Using the Mini-Toolbar to Enhance Text.

As you have already seen, there are several methods available for you to enhance text. In this portion of the lesson, you will use one more, the mini-toolbar. When you select text the mini-toolbar automatically appears in the background just above the selected text. You can activate the mini-toolbar by moving into it. You will now use the mini-toolbar to bold and underline a word.

1.   In the first line of the first paragraph, select the word *easily*.

You should now see the mini-toolbar in the background just above the selected word.

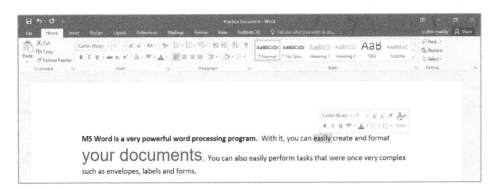

2.   Click the Bold and Underline tools on the mini-toolbar.
The word *easily* should now be boldfaced and underlined.

Using Keyboard Shortcuts to Enhance Text.

Your head may be spinning now seeing so many ways to enhance text. But, before you give up in frustration, here is one more method. This purpose of doing this is to show you again, that there are a variety of ways to perform most commands. Keyboard shortcuts provide a very quick way to perform commands when your hands are on the keyboard.

So, to give you an idea of how this works, we will have you select and underline a word using only the keyboard.

1.   Move to the beginning of the document with (Control+Home).

The insertion point should now be at the beginning of this document.

2.   Hold the (Shift) key down and hit the (Down) arrow twice.

The first two lines of this document should be selected. Holding down the Shift key selects text when you move using the keyboard.

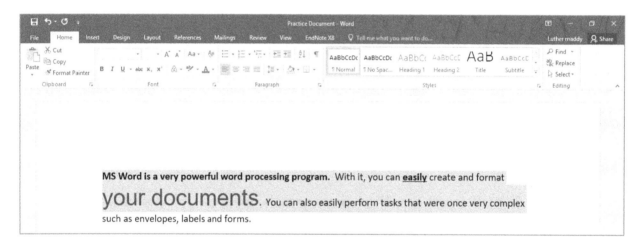

3.   With these two lines selected, press (Control+U).

Control+U is the keyboard shortcut for underlining.

4.   Press (Down) again to de-select this text.

Are you confused yet?
Let's take a break and let the spinning in your head slow down. You've just seen several ways to do the same thing. This was not done to confuse you, but to simply make you aware that there are a variety of ways to perform some commands.

When there are several methods available, there is no one right way. The way that you can remember is the right way. There is no reason to try to memorize every possible way to do every command in Word. Instead, learn the method that appeals the most to you and get very comfortable with that method. As you become more comfortable with Word in general, you can increase your productivity by learning additional, perhaps faster ways to perform the commands that you use the most.

Using Save As instead of Save

When you use the Save command, the document changes are saved under the original file name. This lets you add to the document as you make changes or add text.

Sometimes, you may wish to keep the original document as it was and also save the changes. In this case, you would use the Save As command to make a new document (file) from the document on your screen. The original remains unaltered as long as you did not use the Save command after making changes.

In this portion of this lesson you will create a new document from the changed version of the document you are currently working with. The original will remain as it was before you started making changes.

1.   **Choose the Save As command from the File menu.**

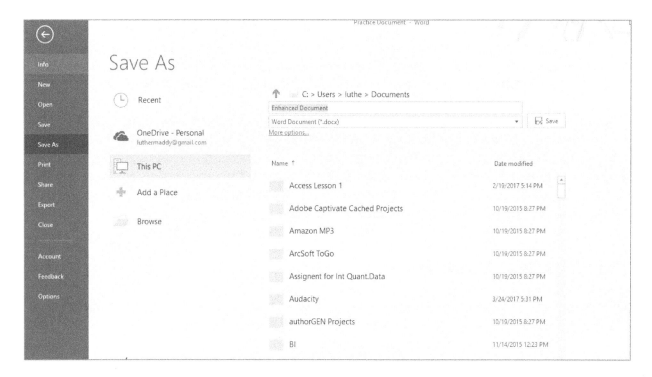

2. Click the current folder option, Documents as shown in the example.

You are choosing to store this new document in the same folder you placed the document it was based on, *Practice Document.*

Word will now display the Save As dialog box. You have seen this before, when you first saved this document. Now, you just need to give this revised version a different name.

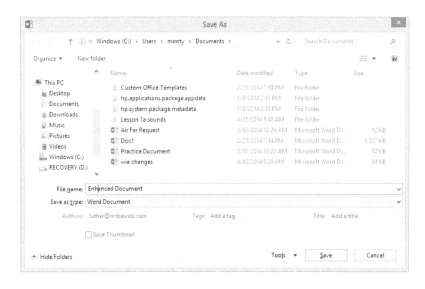

3. Type *Enhanced Document* in the File name text box and click Save to save this revised file with the new name.

© 2017 Luther M. Maddy III

4.   Open the File menu and choose Close to close this document.

Enhancing New Text

So far in this lesson you have only changed or enhanced existing text. To do this you had to select the text you wanted to change, and then tell Word how to change that text. Only the text you selected changed.

In this portion of the exercise, you will create a new document, formatting and enhancing it, as you create it. To have the next text appear with an enhancement, you will turn on the feature you want and then type the text. When you do not want that formatting option anymore, turn it off. Once you turn on an enhancement, it will stay on until you turn it off.

1.   Choose the New command in the File menu and click create a new blank document.

You can also create a new document very quickly with the keyboard shortcut (Control+N).

You should now have a new, blank document. You will now change the font size before you begin typing.

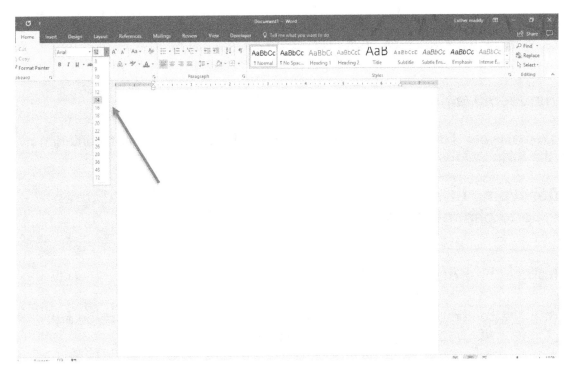

2.   Use the Font Size tool on the Home tab of the Ribbon to change the font to 14 points.

This time you are using the tools on the Ribbon to change font attributes rather than the Font dialog box as you did previously. Neither of these methods is superior but, if the feature you want is available with a tool on the Ribbon, that is probably the fastest way to access that feature.

As you click the drop-down list button on this tool you can select from many pre-set font sizes, the larger the number the larger the font size. One point is approximately 1/72nd of an inch; therefore 72 points would mean the letters would be approximately 1 inch tall. This varies somewhat by font style, but is a close approximation.

3.   Click the Center tool in the Paragraph group of the Home tab to change the alignment to Center.

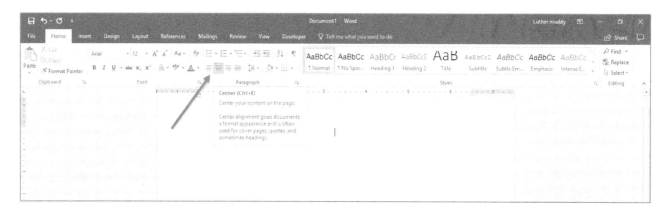

You should notice that the insertion point moved to the center of the line. Word will automatically center what you type next. The centered text will be the heading of a memo you are going to create.

4.   Type *Memorandum* and press (Enter) twice.

Centering remains on. To return to left aligned text you will have to turn off centering by selecting the Align Left tool.

5.   After typing this text, click the Align Left tool in the Paragraph group to change the alignment back to Left.

6.   Change the Font Size to 12 points.

We only want the centered heading to be larger than the rest of the text, so you are changing the font size back to the commonly used 12 point size.

Now you are going to create the text for this memo. This memo will incorporate Boldfacing, Underlining and Strikethrough text enhancements. As you create this text you will "turn on" an enhancement when you want to use it and "turn off" the enhancement when done. You can find Bold, Underline and Strikethrough tools on the Home tab of the ribbon.

7. **Now, use the Bold, Italic, Strikethrough, and Underline options from the Ribbon and the Font dialog box launcher from the font group to create the memo as shown:**

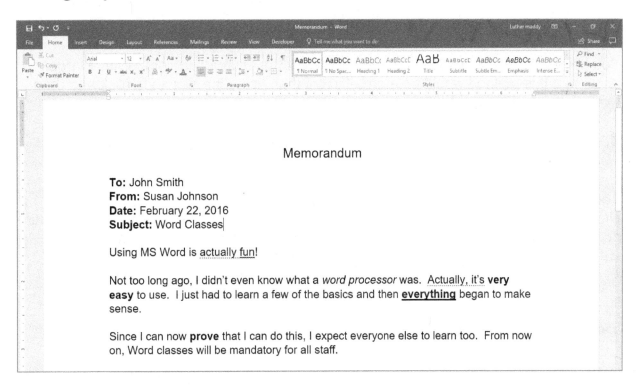

 Hint: Some formatting options work like toggle switches. When you are finished using an enhancement such as Boldfacing, click the same tool to turn off the feature!

The memo text above was not shown shaded, even though you are typing it so that you could see the enhancements.

8. **When done, save this document as *Memorandum,* then close the document.**

Removing Enhancements

To remove text enhancements such as bold, italic, or font style or size changes, begin by selecting the text you want changed. Then, with the text selected, turn off the options you do not want. If you want to remove all of one type of enhancement, such as boldfacing throughout an entire document, you can select the entire document and then "turn off" boldfacing. This is what you will do in the next portion of this exercise.

1.   **Open the *Memorandum* document**

2.   **Select the entire document with (Control+A).**

You have just used a keyboard shortcut to select the entire document. With a large document this method would be more efficient than using the mouse to click and drag through the entire document.

3.   **Click <u>twice</u> on the Bold, Underline and Italic tools on the Home tab of the ribbon.**

You have now removed all the bold, italic, and underlining from this document. You click each of the tools twice because the first time, Word applied that option to the entire document. The second time, it removed that option from the entire document.

4.   **Save and close the *Memorandum* document.**

The Clear Formatting Option

Word also has a clear formatting option that you can use to quickly remove all formatting. To use this option:

1.   **Open Enhanced Document, then select the entire document with Control+A.**

2.   **On the Home tab, click the Styles dialog box launcher (the ⌐ to the right of Styles) to display the styles drop down list.**

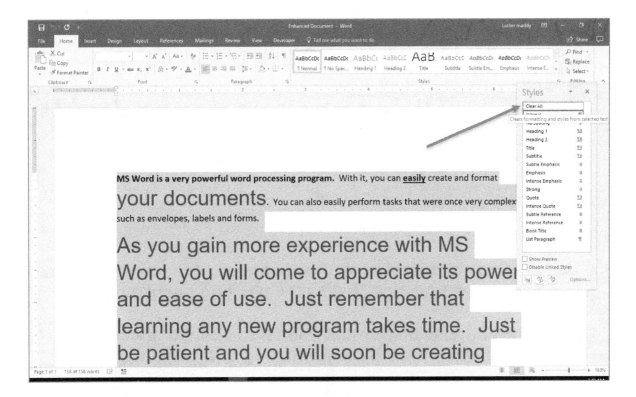

3. **Select Clear All in the styles list.**

At this point, all formatting from the selected text will be removed.

4. **Close the Styles list by clicking the X at the top right of the list.**

3. **Save and close the document.**

Skill Builder Lesson #3

1. **Open Airfare Request.**

2. **Move to the top of the document. Create two new blank lines at the top. Then, move back to the top, turn on centering, change the font to 14 points and type:**

   No Fault Travel Agency
   143 San Andreas Fault Line
   Hollister, CA 93992

3. **Use the Copy and Paste commands to copy the company name, "No Fault Travel Agency" below the booking agent's name.**

4. **After copying, use the Format Painter to change the copied company name to match the formatting of the agent's title.**

5. **Change the company name at the top of the letter to be Arial font, 24 points and Blue.**

Your document should now appear like that below.

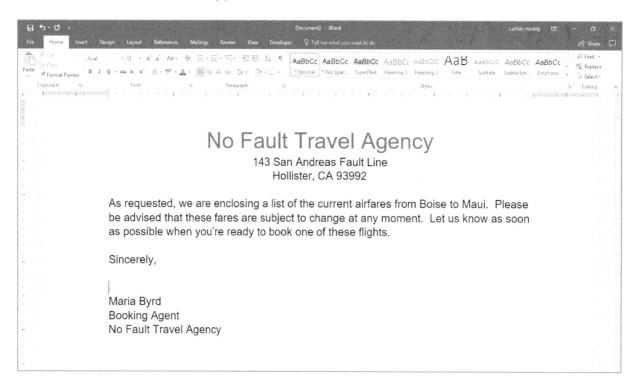

6. **Save and close this file.**

Lesson #4: Basic Paragraph and Page Formatting

In this lesson you will learn to:

Change Document Margins
Change Line Spacing
Create Hanging Indents
Indent Paragraphs
Use Tab Stops

Lesson #4: Basic Paragraph and Page Formatting

In the previous lesson you changed the appearance of the text (words) within the document. In this lesson you will focus on changing the layout of entire pages and paragraphs in the document. Layout changes include the top, bottom, left and right margins and features like line spacing and paragraph indentation. In addition to these features, this lesson will also have you explore tab setting, which is a feature that lets you quickly put information in single spaced columns.

Page Layout

In Word, many formatting options are available in the Page Layout tab. Here you can change document margins, paper size, orientation and other document options. In this exercise you'll select a few of these options to become familiar with their use.

1. **Use the File menu to create a New Blank Document.**

You can also use the keyboard shortcut of (Control+N) to create a new document. You do not need to memorize the entire list of keyboard shortcuts. However, as you become more comfortable with Word you will find that you can be more productive by learning a few shortcuts for the commands you use often.

2. **Right-click the Status bar and turn on Vertical Page Position if it is not already on. Click in the text area to close this menu when done.**

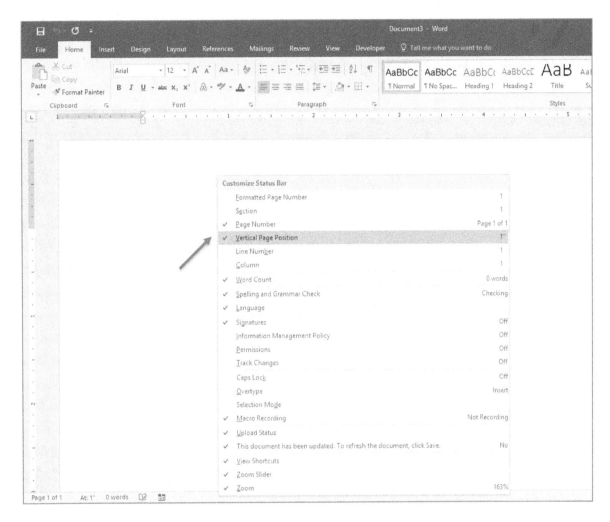

When you examine the status bar now you should see *At: 1"*. This shows you that the insertion point is 1" below the top edge of the printed paper. This represents the current top margin setting.

You will now going change the page margins for this document. With a smaller top margin, text will be positioned closer to the top of the printed page. The next document you create will include a letterhead which is usually closer than 1" to the top edge of the page.

In cases where you are using preprinted letterhead, you will likely want to make the top margin larger. Otherwise the text you type be printed over the letterhead instead of below it. To find out what your margin settings should be, grab a ruler and measure from the top edge of the page to the place below the letterhead where you want your text to begin.

3.   Click the Layout tab on the Ribbon.

4. Click the Margins tool and choose Custom Margins.

While there are many pre-set margin options you can choose from, the Custom Margins dialog box lets you set exactly the margins you want. When you are using Word for your own documents, you may often be table to use one of the pre-set margin settings. By default, Word 2016's margins are 1" all around the edges of the page.

You should now see the Page Setup dialog box which allows you to specify the exact margin settings you want.

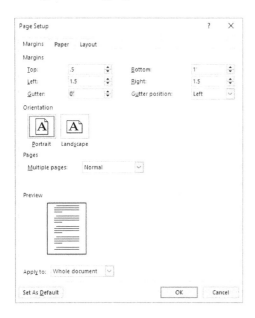

5.   Change the Top margin to .5".

You can press (Tab) to move from field to field within this dialog box. When you are in the correct field, just type the value you want.

6.   Change the Left and Right margins to *1.5*" each.

Leave the bottom margin set at 1".

7.   When done, click OK.

Since you are, or should be, in Print Layout view, you will see the margin changes reflected on both ruler bars. If the horizontal ruler is not visible in the Print Layout view, click the View tab and turn on the Ruler option on the ribbon. After making this change, the Status bar displays at .5", reflecting the new margin setting.

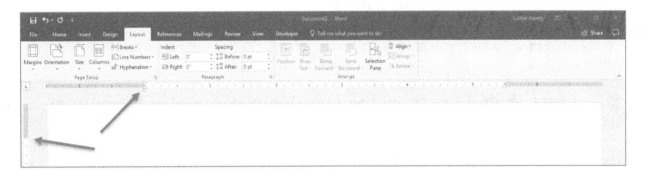

8.   Click the Home tab and change the alignment to Center (use the Center tool on the Ribbon) and type:

No Fault Travel Agency
143 San Andreas Fault Line
Hollister, CA 93992

9.   On the line below the zip code, change the alignment back to Left and then press (Enter) one more time.

If the line with the city, state and zip code lost centering, make sure you are on the line below before changing the alignment back to Left. Pressing (Enter) twice creates two blank lines between the letterhead and the text you are about to create.

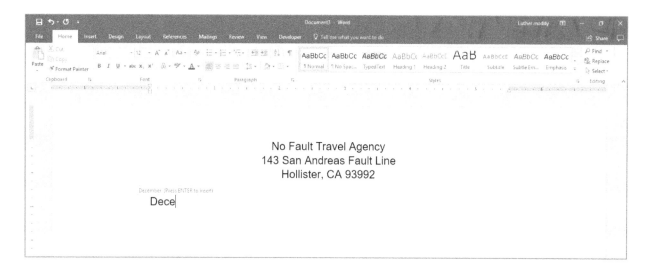

10. **Type the first four letters of the current month such as *Dece* for December or *Janu* for January.**

You should now see a box displaying the current month's entire name above the letters you just typed,

11. **Press (Enter) to accept the AutoComplete entry of the current month.**

The AutoComplete feature will only work for months that have more than five letters.

12. **After the current month is complete, press (Space). You should now see another AutoComplete box with the current date displayed above the text you are typing, press (Enter) to insert the entire date.**

The date you see on the examples in this workbook will be different than the current date. Use the current date rather than the date in the following example pages.

13. **Press (Enter) to accept this date. Press (Enter) again to move one line down the page.**

14.   Two lines below the date, type the following:

Mr. and Mrs. Martin Johnson
343 Overland Dr.
Boise, ID 83709

Dear Mr. and Mrs. Johnson,

15.   Create two new blank lines below the salutation by pressing (Enter).

Paragraph Formatting

As with text enhancements, after you turn on a paragraph formatting feature, the text you type after turning that feature on will appear with that formatting option. To change existing paragraphs, you must first select the paragraphs you want to change. Then, with the text selected, choose the Paragraph formatting options you want.

For this portion of the lesson you will use the Paragraph dialog box. You will use this to change paragraph indentation and line spacing.

1.   Open the Paragraph dialog box by clicking the dialog box launcher (   ) at the bottom right of Paragraph group on the Home tab.

You should now see the Paragraph dialog box. You will use this dialog box to change the line spacing to double. You could have also used the Line Spacing tool on the Ribbon. The Paragraph dialog box allows you to change many additional settings.

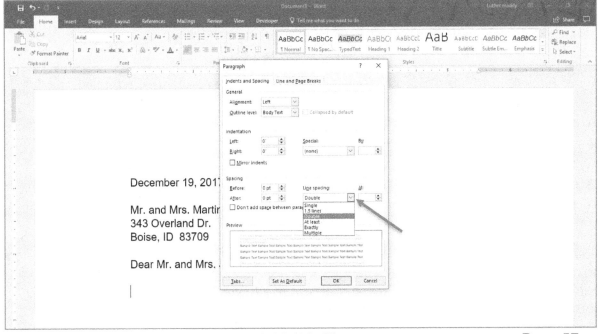

2.   In the Paragraph dialog box, click the Line spacing drop down list button and choose Double as the line spacing.

Spacing Between Paragraphs

You have been adding blank lines between paragraphs by pressing the (Enter) key. Word can do this for you automatically. It does this with the Paragraph Spacing option. If you examine the Paragraph dialog box you'll see the Spacing section here. You should also notice there is a setting for Before and After a paragraph. There may already be a default (automatic) setting here. For example, Word may already be inserting 10 points after each paragraph. Setting automatic spacing after a paragraph is helpful and eliminates you having to press (Enter) between each paragraph. However, while you're learning Word, we're going to have you ensure this setting to 0 points so that each blank line only occurs when you press enter.

3.   In the Paragraph spacing section, ensure that both the Before and After are set to 0.

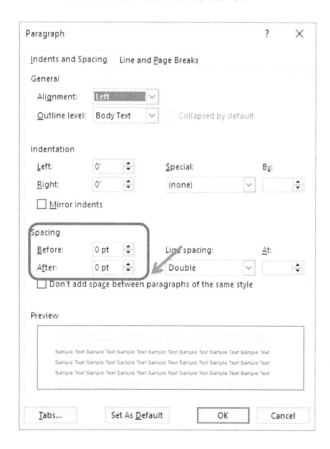

You should also notice the *Set As Default* button at the bottom of the Paragraph dialog box. If you click this button, any changes you have made here will be applied automatically when you create new documents. We won't have you do this until you learn a little more about Word and the options you want to make automatic.

4.   Click OK to close the Paragraph dialog box.

From this point on, all text you type will be double spaced until you change this setting back to Single. And, if you thought this was the only way to change line spacing you should know better by now. You can also change the line spacing very easily with the Ribbon on the Paragraph group of the Home tab and you'll use that method as well later.

5.   Type the following paragraph, and press (Enter) when done:

We just wanted to let you know that your trip to Bangkok, Thailand is coming together nicely. We have scheduled several trips and tours that will enable you to see much of this beautiful country. In the following paragraphs you'll find some important information about your trip.

This paragraph should be double spaced. Now, you will use another method to change the line spacing back to single.

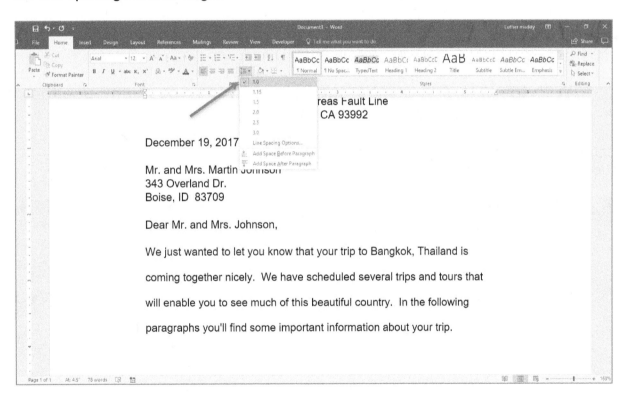

6.   Make sure the insertion point is below the last paragraph, then click the Line Spacing tool on the Ribbon and change the line spacing back to Single.

Indenting Paragraphs

If you wish to offset one or more paragraphs from the text around it, you can indent that text. The Indent command will cause the entire paragraph to move to the right, rather than just the first line, as it would if you pressed the (Tab) key before typing the paragraph.

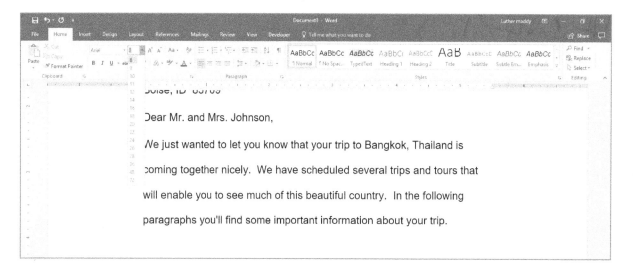

7.   With the insertion point at the bottom of the document, use the Ribbon and change the Font Size to 8 points.

Depending on the font you are currently using, your lines may not break exactly as shown in this example.

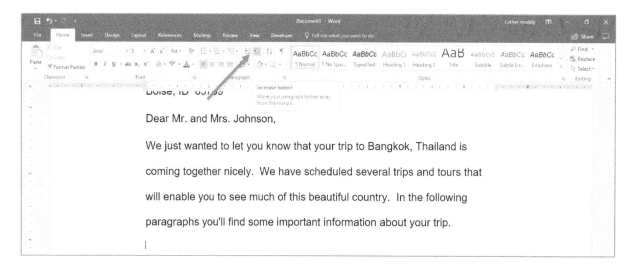

8.   Locate and click the Increase Indent tool on the Ribbon one time to indent the next paragraph.

Each time you click the Increase Indent tool it indents 0.5" to the right. If you wanted to indent this paragraph 1", you would click this tool twice.

© 2017 Luther M. Maddy III

9.   Now, type the following paragraph and press (Enter) when done:

Remember that any problems you have on your trip will not be our fault. We will not be held responsible for any loss of life, limb or luggage. You assume all risks yourself.

Notice that the entire paragraph is indented. If you wanted to indent a paragraph after you already typed it, just select the text and click the Indent tool.

10.   After typing this paragraph, change the Font size back to 12 points and press (Enter) key to create a blank line after this paragraph.

Just like many other commands that affect the appearance of text, the Indent command stays "on" until you turn it off. If you do not change the indent level back to the original setting, all additional text will be indented.

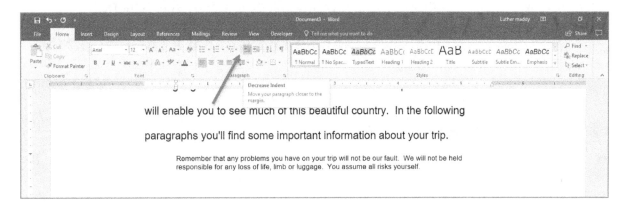

11.   Click the Decrease Indent tool to end paragraph indentation.

You will find the Decrease Indent tool just to the left of the Increase Indent tool. This tool also decreases the indentation in increments of 0.5" each time you click it.

12.   Turn on Underlining and type: *Your Itinerary:*

13.   Turn off Underlining and then press (Enter) twice.

This is the only text you want underlined. Remember formatting changes, once turned on, stay on until you turn them off.

Hanging Indents

Word has different indentation styles. Hanging indents are useful for bulleted or numbered paragraphs or when manually creating a bibliography. There is no default tool for the hanging indent command. You can create hanging indents from the

Paragraph dialog box or even using the ruler. However, the easiest way to turn this feature on is with the keyboard shortcut (Control+T).

1. Press (Control+T) twice.

Like the left indent command, the hanging indent uses increments of 0.5". Each time you pressed Control+T, the left indent marker on the ruler moved 0.5".

2. Now, type *5/1/19* and press (Tab).

When you press (Tab) the insertion point will move to the bottom indentation mark. All lines of text within the paragraph you are typing will now indent at this mark.

3. Type the following paragraph and notice that it "hangs" off the date.

Arrive in Bangkok at 11:45 p.m. Next, you'll travel to your hotel and check in. After checking in you will begin your tour of the countryside.

Notice that when you pressed enter after this paragraph, the insertion point returned to the left margin. You should also see that the paragraph "hung" off the date.

4. Type the following two paragraphs by typing the date first, then pressing (Tab ➔) before typing the text. Use the (Enter) key to insert blank lines between these paragraphs.

5/2/17   Recover from jetlag. Do nothing.

5/3/17   Leave Bangkok and return home.

Notice that you did not need to execute the hanging indent command for each hanging paragraph. Once you turned this feature "on", it stays until you turn it "off".

5. With the insertion point below the last date line, press (Control+Shift+T) twice, until you see the paragraph indent marks both return to the Left margin on the horizontal ruler.

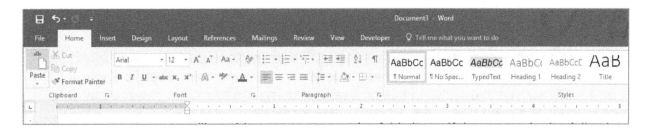

This turns "off" the hanging indent feature.

6.   Now two lines below the last itinerary entry, type the following text:

Thank you for choosing No Fault Travel. Please call if you have any questions.

Cynthia Anderson
Booking Agent

Your document should now appear similar to the one below:

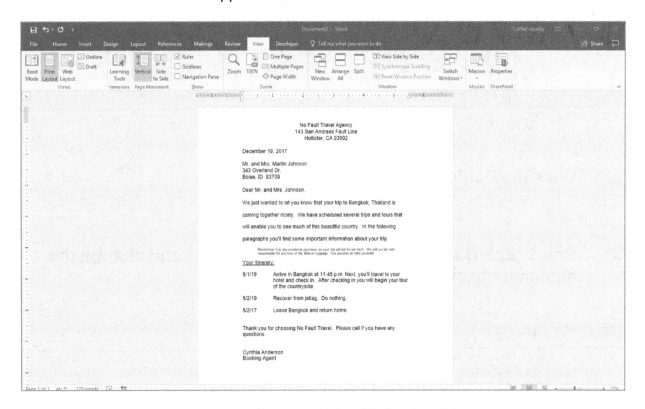

7.   Save this file as *Johnson Confirmation Letter* and close it.

Setting Tabs

Tab setting is very easy in Word. You use tab stops to place portions of your text in single spaced columns. You can also place text in columns using Word's Table feature. You'll learn about tables later in this course, but using tab stops, as you are about to see is easy and even has some advantages over using Tables.

You can use the Ruler bar if you only need basic tab settings. You will also learn to add dots or other characters between the tabular columns in this lesson.

Setting tab stops is more efficient than pressing the (Space) bar numerous times after completing the text in one column and moving to the next column, which is extremely more productive. When you set a tab stop, you move the next column with only one keystroke, the Tab key. Setting tabs also ensures the columns will be perfectly aligned, which is difficult if not impossible when you just use the (Space) bar to create columned text.

Word allows several different types of tabs to be set, depending on the alignment you would like.

1.   Use the File menu to create a New Blank Document.

2.   Click the Center tool on the Ribbon and type:

Table of Contents

3.   Press (Enter) to move one line down the page and change the alignment back to left alignment.

Using the Ruler Bar to Set Tabs

To set tabs on the Ruler bar, you simply click on the horizontal ruler where you want the tab stops to be set. You do not need to worry about deleting the existing tab stops, which occur every 0.5". Word automatically erases the default tab stops as soon as you place your own tab on the Ruler.

Word allows you to set left, right, center, and decimal table which control the alignment of the text at that tab stop. You can use the Tab button at the very left edge of the horizontal ruler to change the tab type.

© 2017 Luther M. Maddy III

Before you set tabs, we will have you check some paragraph settings to make sure they do not interfere with this portion of the lesson.

1.   **Click the paragraph dialog box launcher to display the paragraph dialog box.**

It is possible to set tabs within this dialog box, but for this exercise you will use the Ruler. For tab stops to work properly, you must ensure that you have all other indentation options turned off.

2.   **In the Paragraph dialog box, ensure both the Left and Right indentations are set at 0". Also, ensure the Special option displays "none".**

3.   **Click OK to leave the paragraph dialog box.**

You are now ready to set tab stops using the Ruler.

4.   **Make sure the Horizontal ruler is displayed. Click on tab button at the far left edge of the Ruler until it displays a Left Tab indicator as shown in the example.**

Release the mouse button after clicking on the tab button.

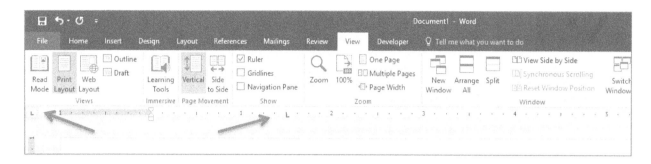

When you point to the tab stop type button on the ruler bar you should notice the tool tip informing you that this button represents a left tab. If it says something other than left, click this button until the symbol changes to appear as an "L", representing a Left Tab. Setting a left tab means the text you type using this tab stop will begin (be left aligned) at the tab stop. You will see some other tab stops in action as you continue with this lesson.

5. Now, carefully click at the 1.5" mark on the horizontal Ruler.

You have now set a tab stop at this location. This is verified with the "L" mark on the ruler at this position. If you do not set the tab exactly where it should be, you can move it by carefully dragging it to the correct location.

If you attempt to move a tab marker to another location, make sure you click precisely on the tab stop marker on the ruler. If not, you may find that you have set an additional, incorrectly placed tab stops. In that case you can click on the extra tab and drag it down, off the ruler to remove it. You are setting a Left tab, not because it is on the left of the page, but because you want the information in this column to be left aligned at the tab stop.

6. Move the mouse pointer back to the tab selector button at the left edge of the Ruler bar.

7. Click on the tab stop type twice, until it shows that you will be setting a Right Tab.

The right tab displays as a backwards "L".

8. After selecting the Right tab stop, click at 4.75" on the Ruler bar to set a right tab at this location.

You selected a Right tab because the information in this column is to be right aligned at the tab stop.

9.   Now, pressing (Tab➔) and then type *Getting Started*.

10.   Next, press (Tab➔) again and type *1*.
You should notice the insertion point jumped to the tab stop each time you pressed (Tab).

11.   Press (Enter) and then type the following text, pressing (tab) before each topic and then again before typing the page number.

(Tab) *Basic Editing* (Tab) *5*
(Tab) *Formatting* (Tab)   *10*
(Tab) *Moving & Copying* (Tab) *22*
(Tab) *Auto Text* (Tab) *30*

Your document should now appear like the illustration below. Notice the difference in the alignment of the text columns due to the tab type set for each.

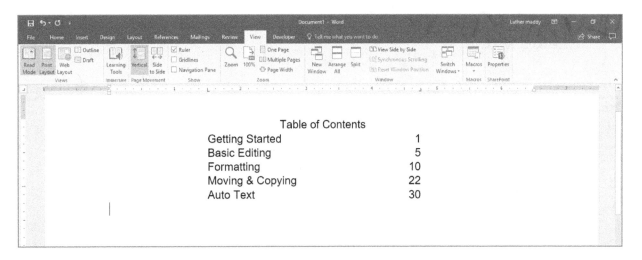

Using Tab Leaders
Word allows you to select a variety of leaders between tabbed columns. You can choose from dots, dashes or solid lines. To set leaders, you will enter the Tabs dialog box from the Paragraph dialog box. To add leaders to existing text, as you will do here, you will need to select the text you want to change first.

1.   Use the keyboard to move to the beginning of "Getting Started" in the tabbed information.

Be careful not to select the blank line above or below the tabbed information.

2.   Press and hold the Shift key. Then move to the end of the last page number with the (Down) arrow.

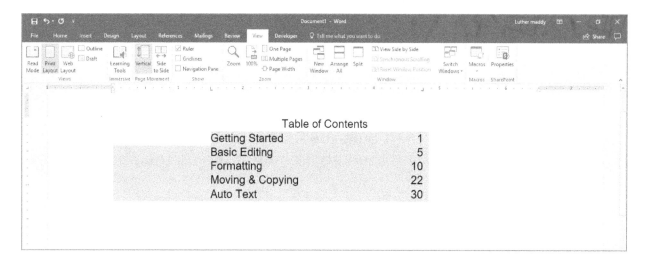

You have used the keyboard to select this text for accuracy.

3.   Display the Home tab and then launch the Paragraph dialog box (click [ ]) and click the Tabs ... button at the bottom left of this dialog box.

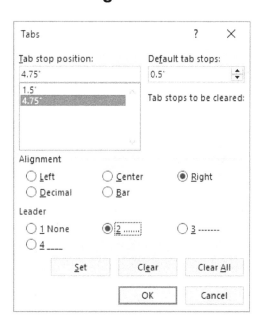

4.   In the Tabs dialog box, click on 4.75" in the Tab stop positions section of this dialog box.

If you did not set your tab exactly at 4.75" you will see a different value here but that will not matter. Simply select the second tab in the list. If you have more than two tabs set here, you can click on the one you do not want and click the Clear button to remove it.

5.   Next, click Leader option #2.

You have chosen to place dots between the columns. If you are making more than one change you would need to click Set after each change. This is not necessary this time because you have made only one change.

6.   Click OK when done.

You should now see leaders between the columns you just created. Tab leaders come before the tab stop you apply them to. This is why you selected the second, 4.75" tab location before selecting the leaders. If you had selected the first tab, the leaders would have appeared before the first column of text.

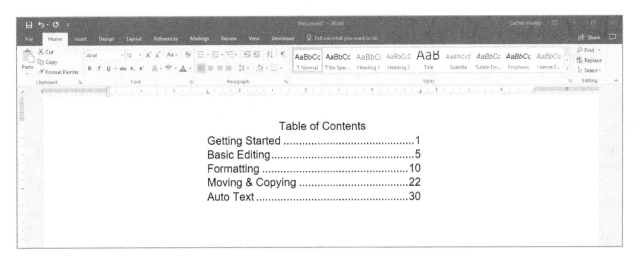

Adjusting Tabs with the Ruler Bar

To move a tab, just drag it to the desired location on the Ruler bar. If you want to change existing text, make sure you select that text first. To remove a Tab, drag it off the ruler bar and into the document window.

1.   Move to the end of the document. Make sure you are below the last line in the tabbed columns.

2.   Carefully click the tab marker at 1.5" and drag it into the text to remove it. Do the same with the tab at 4.75".

The two tab stops you set should now be removed and Word defaulted back to a left tab every 0.5".

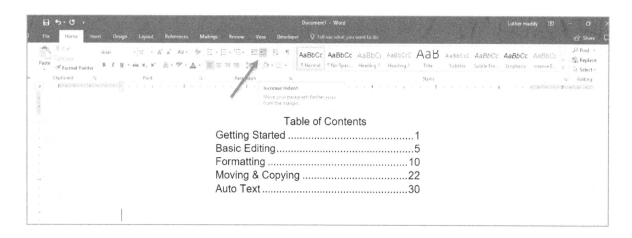

3. **With the insertion point two lines below the last line in the tabbed columns, click the Increase Indent tool on the Ribbon once. Next type:**

The Increase Indent tool makes it very easy to indent single paragraphs. When you are creating new text, the indent command stays on until you turn it off.

4. **Two lines below this paragraph. Click the Decrease Indent tool in the Paragraph group. Next, type the following paragraph:**

When you no longer want your paragraphs indented, click the Decrease Indent tool.

Your document should appear similar to the one below. Your lines may break differently depending on the font you are using.

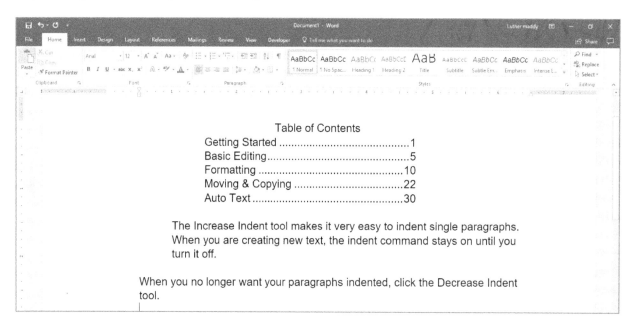

5. **When done, save this file as *Tab Practice* and Close it.**

1.   **Open Airfares Request.**

2.   **Change the Top Margin to 0.5".**

3.   **Move to a line above the letter closing. Make sure you have at least 1 blank line, (press Enter), between the paragraphs and the closing line.**

4.   **Next, set a left aligned tab at 1.5" and a decimally aligned tab at 4.75" on the ruler bar. Then, type the following using the appropriate Tabs ➔:**

  ➔   SouthWest   ➔   225.00
  ➔   United ➔   444.00
  ➔   Delta   ➔   1019.00
  ➔   Value Jet   ➔   89.00

5.   **After creating the airfare list, add dot leaders between the columns.   (Hint: Paragraph to Tabs)**

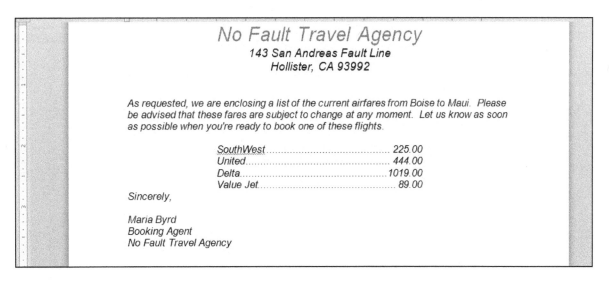

6.   **Save and close the file.**

Lesson #5: Envelopes & Labels
In this lesson you will learn to:

Create Envelopes and Labels from Letters
Create an Entire Sheet of Labels

Lesson #5: Envelopes and Labels

It is very easy to create either envelopes or labels from letters you have written. In this exercise, you will open a previously created letter and create an envelope to use for mailing that letter. After creating the envelope, you will create an entire sheet of labels with *No Fault Travel's* return address.

Creating Envelopes

To create an envelope, first write the letter. Then, open the Mailings tab and select Labels in the Create Group. Word will then automatically pull the mailing address from the letter and place it on the envelope.

1.   **Open *Johnson Confirmation Letter.***

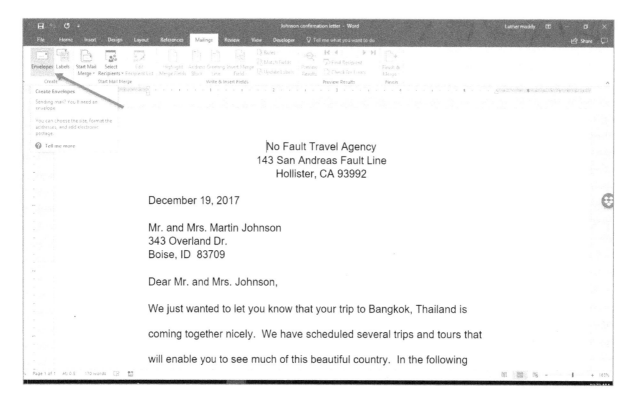

2.   **Click the Envelopes tool from the Mailings tab.**

You should now see the Envelopes and Labels dialog box.

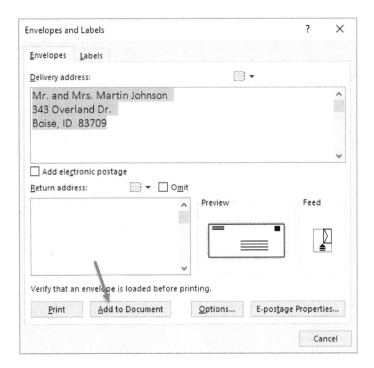

Word automatically copies the mailing address for this letter into the Envelopes and Labels dialog box. Rather than printing, you will add the envelope to your letter so you can change the case of the address. After adding it to the document, you could also change fonts, add graphic images, or add other enhancements to the envelope.

3.   In the Envelope dialog box, click Add to Document.

You should now see that Word has added the envelope to the top of the letter. You will now capitalize the address using (Shift+F3), the shortcut for this. Placing the address in uppercase lettering will help this envelope meet US Post Office requirements for bulk mailing discounts.

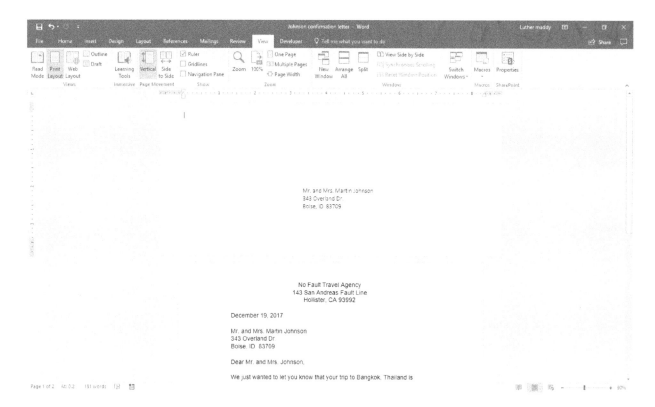

4. Click and drag to select the mailing address in the envelope. With the address selected, press (Shift+F3) to change the mailing address to uppercase.

Any punctuation in the address in the letter will be duplicated on the envelope. If you are receiving bulk mailing discounts, remove the commas and other punctuation. If you do not want to remove punctuation each time you create an envelope, consider omitting the punctuation in the address when you type it in the letter.

Creating Labels

Now you will create an entire sheet of labels with No Fault Travel's return address. You can also create a single label for the delivery address. If you prefer to print labels instead of envelopes, you can tell Word which label to start printing on. This lets you run label sheets through the printer more than once. However, if you do this, use caution and examine the label sheet for loose labels before you do. You may find printing an entire sheet of the same label is practical for mailing addresses if you use them repeatedly.

1.   Move to the top of the letter with (Control+Pagedown). Select the return address at the top i.e. (No Fault Travel).

If Control+Pagedown does not take you to the next page, just move there on your own. A setting may have changed in Word to cause this keystroke shortcut not to work. You will learn to change this setting in a later lesson. Select this text by clicking and dragging, but do so carefully to make sure you do not select portions of the envelope or include the letter's date.

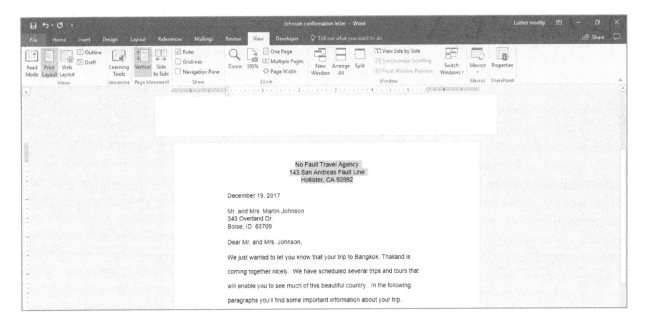

2.   After selecting the return address, click the Labels tool in the Mailings tab.

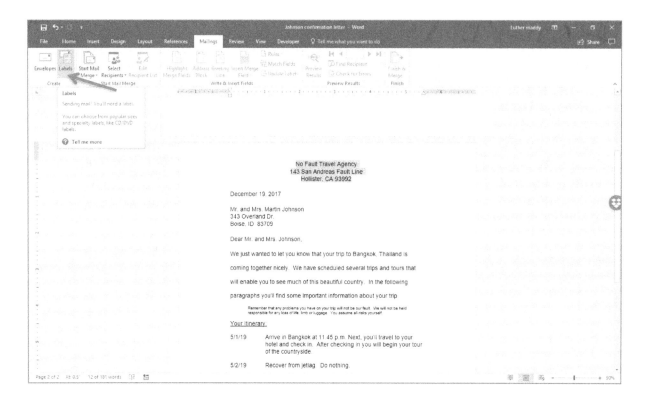

You should now see the labels dialog box. The next step will be to tell Word what kind of labels you are using and whether you want a single label or an entire sheet of the same label.

3. Click the Options button in the Labels dialog box.

You will now need to tell Word what size of label you are using. You can usually do this by specifying the brand of label and that vendor's label number.

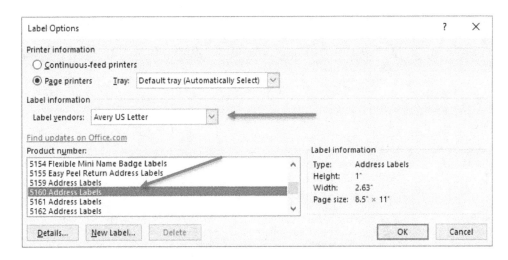

4. **Click the Label vendors drop down box and select Avery US Letter as the vendor. Next, scroll down and select 5160 in the Product number section.**

The label vendor, size, and number you choose when actually using Word may be different, but the labels you have selected represent the "standard" mailing label size. When choosing the label option, if you are not using Avery or some other vendor listed, you can use the size of the label to select the correct label option. Sometimes other vendors will state on the packaging that their label is compatible with "Avery 5160" or some other label number.

5. **After choosing the label type and size, click OK.**

You have now returned to the labels dialog box. Now you need to tell Word if you want to print just one label or an entire sheet of the same label. Since we are printing labels for the company name, select an entire sheet of the same label.

6. **Make sure the Full page of the same label radio button is selected and then click New Document.**

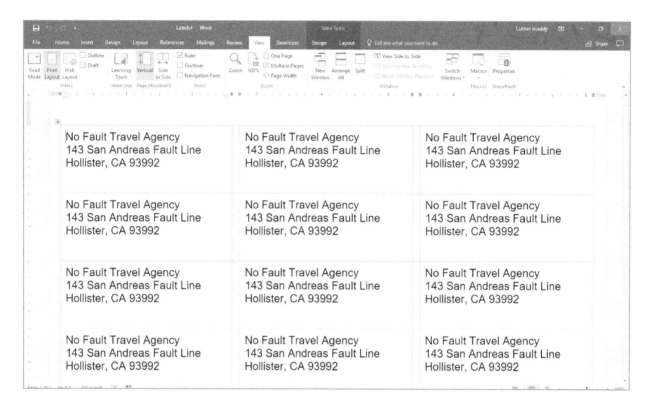

You should now see that Word has created an entire sheet filled with the return address of No Fault Travel. Now that you have this entire sheet of labels, you could easily change the font face or size by first selecting the entire sheet (Control+A) and then choosing the font change.

8.   **Save the labels as *No Fault Return Addresses* and close both files saving changes.**

Skill Builder: Lesson #5

1. Open *Airfare Request*

2. Add the following address below the letterhead:

Ms. Betty Anderson
3829 Abbott St.
Salinas, CA 93906

3. Create an envelope and add it to the document.

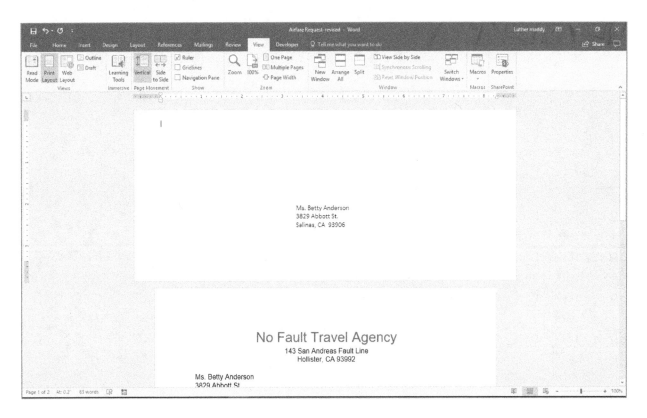

3. Save and close *Airfare Request.*

Lesson #6: Find, Replace and Thesaurus

In this lesson, you will learn to:

Find and Replace Text
Find Synonyms

Lesson #6: Find and Replace

Finding Text

The Find command does what the term implies. It finds text. You can use it as a "go to" command to find a particular heading or phrase quickly in your document.

Replacing Text

The Replace command finds text and lets you change it to something else. This command is useful when you have, for example, consistently misspelled a name throughout the document.

The Replace command provides you the option of replacing every occurrence of the text automatically or choosing which occurrences you want to change and which you do not.

In this exercise you will use the replace command to change the travel agency's name from No Fault Travel to No Fault Travel.

1.   Open the file named *Johnson Confirmation letter.*

The first page of this document is now the envelope you created in the last lesson. You will now move down to the second page, the beginning of the letter itself to being the Find operation.

2.   Move to the top of page 2 (the letter) by pressing (Control+Page Down).

You may recall when you open a document in Word, it always places the insertion point at the beginning of the document. If this shortcut does not take you to the second page, just move there yourself. You will rest this command shortly.

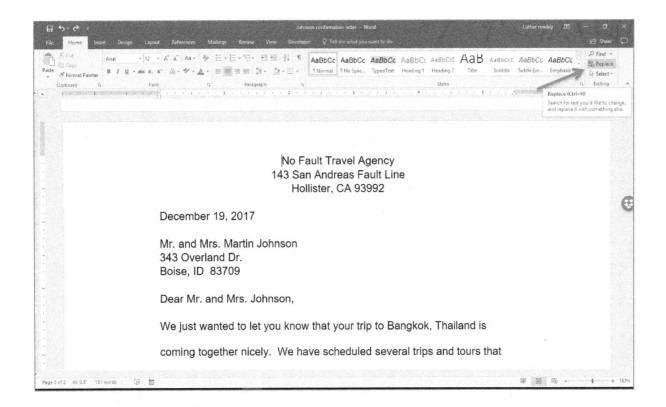

3. **Click the Home tab and then click the Replace tool (far right) on the Ribbon.**

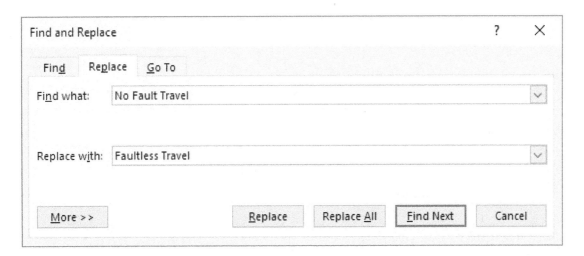

4. **In the Find what section of this dialog box type *No Fault Travel* and press (Tab).**

5. **In the Replace with section of this dialog box, type *Faultless Travel*.**

After specifying the text to find and the replacement text, you then must decide to replace all occurrences, or just the ones you choose. Clicking Replace All will replace every occurrence of No Fault with Faultless.

If you are unsure you want to change every single occurrence, then you would click Find Next. After finding the next occurrence of No Fault Travel in the document you could then choose to replace that one instance by clicking the Replace button. If you do not want to replace that specific occurrence, you would click Find Next to find the next time that text appears in the document.

6.   Click Replace All.

7.   Click OK when Word informs you how many replacements it made. After this, close the Find and Replace dialog box.

You have now effectively changed the name of this company with one command. Scroll through the document to verify that all occurrences of this text have changed.

Using the Thesaurus

The Thesaurus allows you to find synonyms for words appearing in your document. To use the Thesaurus, move the insertion point into the word for which you want to find a synonym. Then, display the Review tab and choose Thesaurus in the Proofing group. You can also quickly display synonyms by right clicking the word.

The Thesaurus will then display synonyms for that word. You then have the option of replacing that word with one of the listed synonyms, or you can lookup synonyms for any of the suggestions.

7.   Move the insertion point into the word *beautiful* and Right-click.

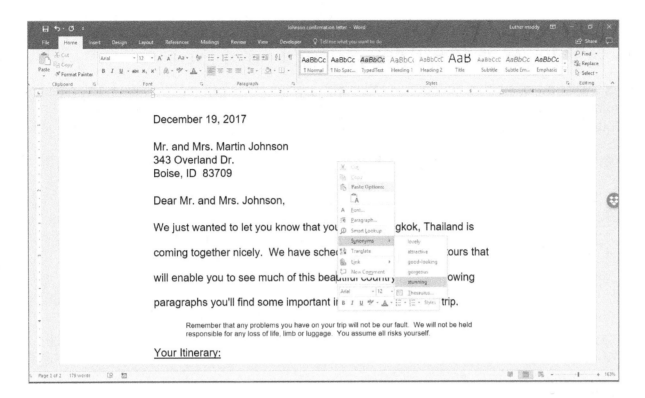

8.   From the sub-menu that appears, choose Synonyms.

You will now choose one of these synonyms.

9.   In the list of Synonyms click on *stunning* to replace the word beautiful with stunning.

After using the find or replace feature, Word changes some shortcut keys. If you try to move from page to page with Control+Pagedown, Word will instead try to execute another find. You can change the browsing keystrokes back to moving page by page rather than repeating the find command by using the Go To… command.

10. With the insertion point anywhere in the letter press (Control+PageUp).

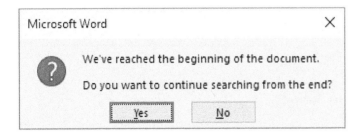

Rather than moving to the top of the previous page, the envelope in this case, Word informed you it repeated the last find command. In this case, this is not what you wanted Word to do with those keystrokes.

11. Click No in the dialog box to inform Word you do not want to perform a search.

Word will now close this dialog box. You will now inform Word that you want to once again use (Control+PageUp) as a command to move page by page through the document, now preform the Find command.

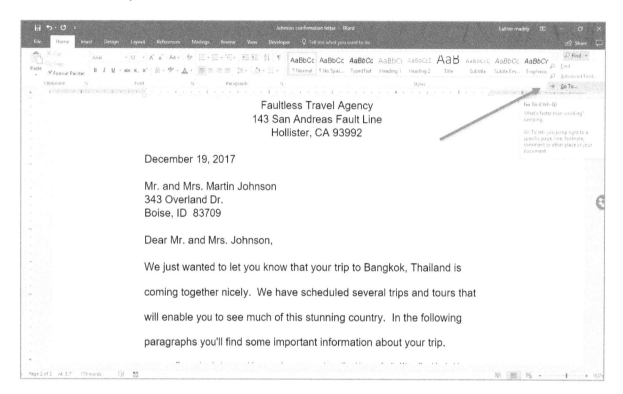

12. Click the drop down list button on the find command and choose Go To... the Goto command.

You could also use the shortcut keys (Control+G) to select the Go To... command.

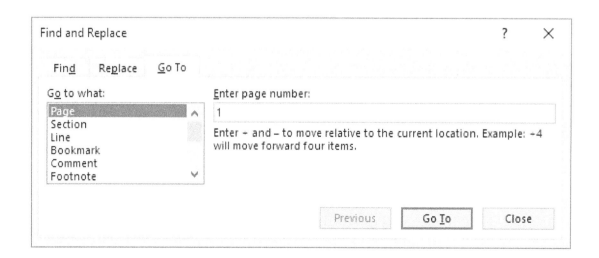

You should see the Find and Replace dialog again, but notice this time the Go To tab is selected. Here you simply enter the page number you wish to move to and then click the Go To button. This is a very quick way to move to a specific page within the document. In this case, you are using this command to change the Control+Pageup and Control+Page Down shortcut keys to page by page rather than repeat the Find command.

13.   Type *1* in the Enter page number text box and click the Go To button.

14.   Click Close to close the Find and Replace dialog box.

You may find that the insertion point stayed on the letter and did not move to the envelope at the top of the document. This is because Word actually numbered the envelope as page 0 rather than page 1. You will learn more about page number in future trainings. For now, check to see if the Control+Pageup and Control+Pagedown commands returned to browsing page by page.

15.   Press (Control+Pageup).

Now, because you changed the function of these keystrokes back to their original setting, you moved up one page. The function of these keystrokes changes every time you use the Find or Replace commands.

16.   Save and close this document.

Skill Builder: Lesson #6

1. **Open *Airfare Request.***

2. **Use the Replace command to change all occurrences of *Maui* to *Hong Kong***

3. **Replace all occurrences of *Value Jet* with *Alaska Airlines.***

4. **Find a suitable synonym for the word *list* in this document.**

5. **Use the Go To command to change the function of the Control+Pageup and Control+Pagedown command back to page browsing.**

6. **Save and close the file.**

Lesson #7: Creating and Formatting Tables

In this lesson, you will learn to:

Insert Tables into Documents
Format Tables
Use Table Styles

Lesson #7: Creating and Formatting Tables

Word tables are very versatile. You can use them to draw attention to a portion of your document. Or, you can use tables as an easy way to put information in columns. You can even use tables to perform basic math operations. In this exercise you will create and then format a table. You will also create cells that compute values.

1. **In a New Document, click the Table tool on the Insert tab. Then, click and drag down and right to create a table of 5 columns and 6 rows.**

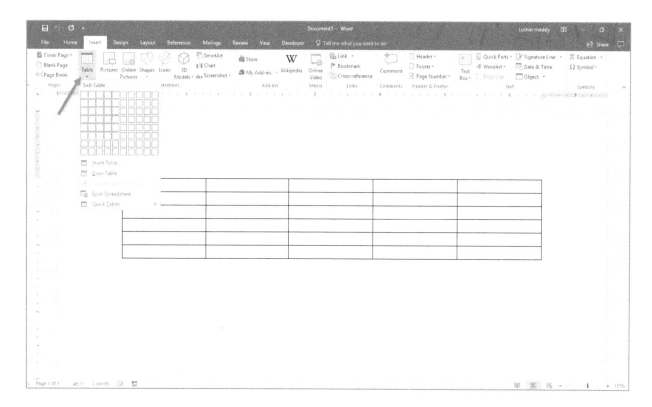

Merging cells

When you create a table, every cell (the intersection of a row and column) is of equal size. You will now merge all the cells in row one to create one large cell for the table's title.

1. **Select all the cells in row 1 of the table you just created.**

You can select all these cells by clicking and dragging across them or by clicking in the selection area (left margin) just to the left of the first column.

2. **After selecting these cells, right-click in the selected cells. From the shortcut menu, choose Merge Cells.**

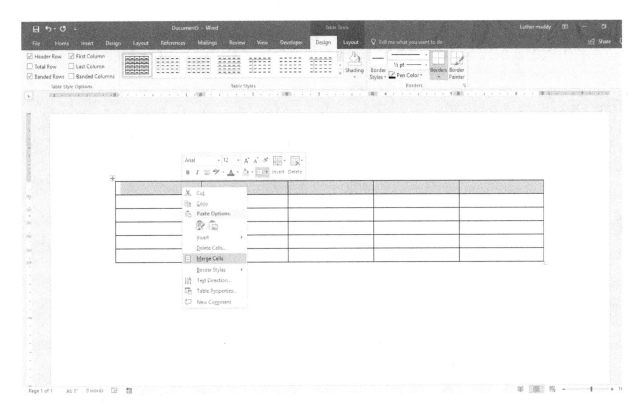

The separation lines between the cells in the first row should disappear. All the cells in row one have merged into one, larger cell.

3.   In the first cell in this table, click the Center tool on the Home tab and type:

# of bookings by location

4.   Press (Tab) to move into the next table cell.

The Tab key moves one cell forward each time you press it. Shift+Tab will move one cell backward.

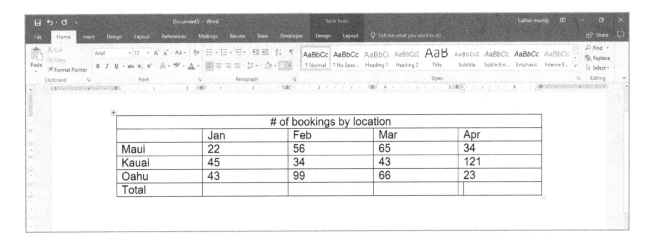

# of bookings by location			
	Jan	Feb	Mar	Apr
Maui	22	56	65	34
Kauai	45	34	43	121
Oahu	43	99	66	23
Total				

5. **Fill in the table as shown in the figure above. Use (Tab) to move forward and (Shift+Tab) to move back cell by cell.**

Inserting rows in a table

You can easily insert new rows in a table. If you need a new row at the end of the table, just press (Tab) in the last cell of the table. Word will then create a new row. If you need to insert rows elsewhere in the table you will use the Insert Row command.

1. **Move into the selection area just to the left of the first row (outside the table) and right-click. From the shortcut menu, choose Insert and then Insert Rows Above.**

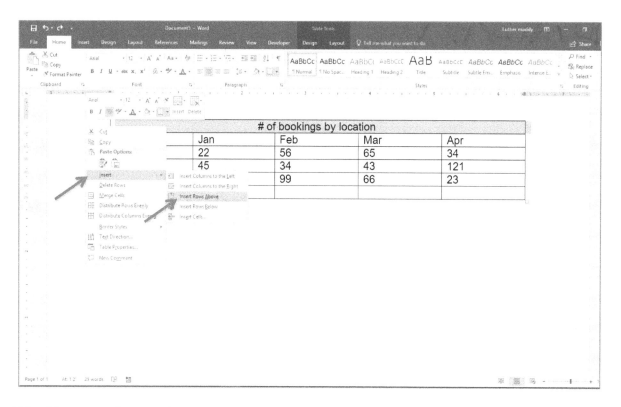

Word has now inserted a new row above the first row. Here you will enter an additional title. When you insert a row, Word will automatically copy the formatting from the row you right-clicked on. You should notice the newly inserted row has already been merged into one large cell.

2. **Move into the new row at the top of the table and type:**

No Fault Travel Hawaii Destinations

Splitting Table Cells

If you need to, you can spilt a cell or cells into more than one cell. You can do this by choosing the Spilt Cell command from the Table menu. You can also do it with the Draw Table tool. In this portion of the exercise, you will use the Draw Table tool.

1.   With the insertion point somewhere in the table, click the Layout tab in the Table Tools section. Then, click the Draw Table tool.

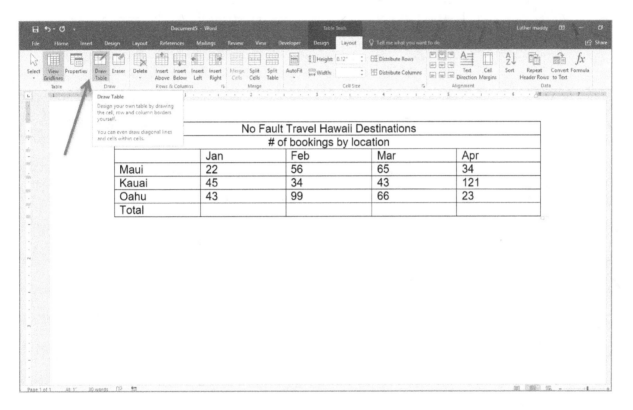

The draw table tool provides a very quick way to split several cells as you are about to do. To do this you simply click and drag where you want to new cells to appear after selecting the Draw Table tool.

2.   Use the Draw Table tool and draw a line to the right of the destinations, beginning in the cell above Maui as shown in the figure below.

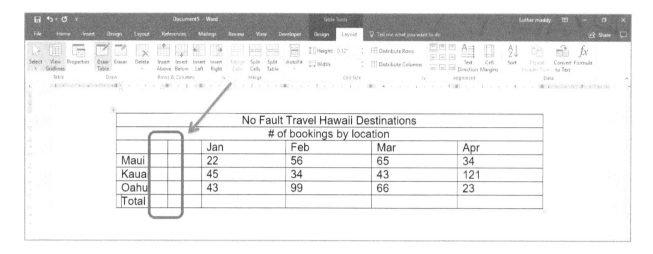

3.   Turn off the Draw Table mode by clicking the Draw Table tool again.

If you don't turn off the draw table tool, Word will attempt to create table cells wherever you click.   You will now merge the new cells you created into one, larger cell.

4.   Select all the cells in the new column you just created.

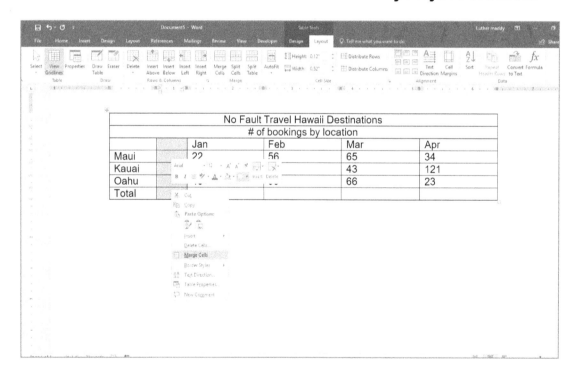

5.   Right-click in the selected cells and chose Merge Cells from the shortcut menu.

7.   In this newly merged cell type: *Island*

Changing Text Direction

The text may not fit well in this cell. You could increase the size of this column to make the text fit. However, you will instead rotate the text to make it fit in the cell. You can change the text direction in a cell easily using the Text Direction tool on the Layout tab.

1. **Staying in the cell where you just typed** *Island,* **display the Layout tab and then click the Change Text direction tool.**

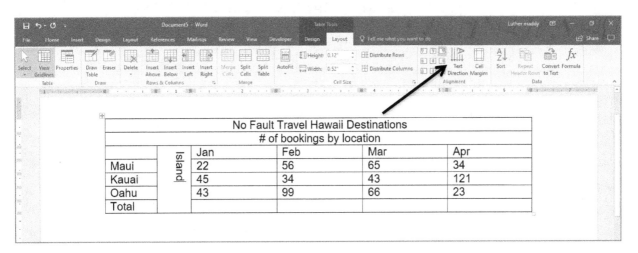

The text in this cell now goes down instead of across in the cell.

2. **Now, click the Center tool on the Home tab.**

The text is now centered vertically in the cell.

Table Cell Alignment

If you examine the cell that contains the word *Island*, you should notice the text is not perfectly aligned in the cell. You have centered the text horizontally, which appears to be centered vertically because of the change in the text direction. Now, you will change the vertical alignment of this cell. And, because of the change in text direction, the change will appear as a horizontal change rather than vertical. However, this should all make sense after you complete the command.

1. **Right-click in the cell containing the word *Island* and choose Table Properties from the shortcut menu.**

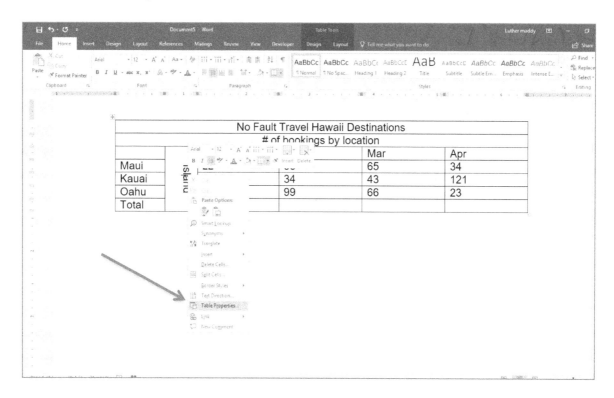

You should now see the table properties dialog box. Here you can change many attributes of the table, rows, columns or individual cells. For now, we'll use this to change the vertical alignment of this cell.

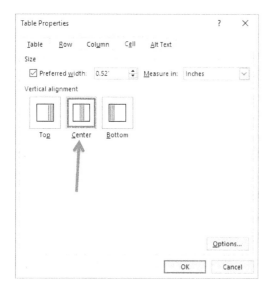

2. **In the Table Properties dialog box, click Cell to display Cell properties. Then, click Center in the Vertical alignment section and click OK.**

 1/18

You should now notice that the text in this cell is centered both horizontally and vertically.

Formatting the Table

You can easily add formatting options to tables. In this portion of the exercise you will change cell alignment, shade rows and rotate text.

1. **Select all the cells that have numbers in them. Select the row that will have totals too as shown.**

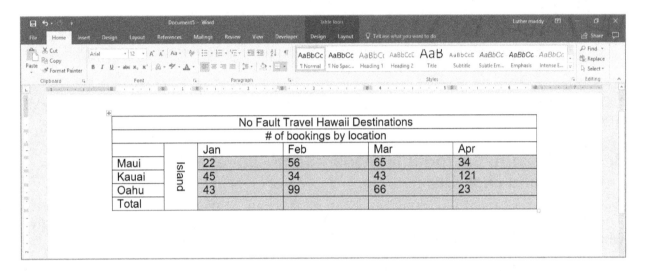

2. **With these cells selected, change the alignment to Right, with (Control+R).**

Of course, you could use another way to change the alignment, such as the Ribbon, and achieve the same results.

Table Formulas

To create formulas in table cells, you can use the Formula option in the Table Layout tab.

1. **Display the Layout tab of the Table Tools, then move into the cell that will display January's total.**

2.   Click the Formula tool on the Layout tab.

You should now see the Formula dialog box. Here you can enter a formula to do basic math within a table cell.

3.   Make sure the formula reads *=Sum(Above)* in the formula text box and click OK.

This formula tells Word to add up all the numbers above it, which in this case is exactly what you want this formula to do.

4.   Move to the bottom of the next column and click the Formula and then OK to enter the same formula there too.

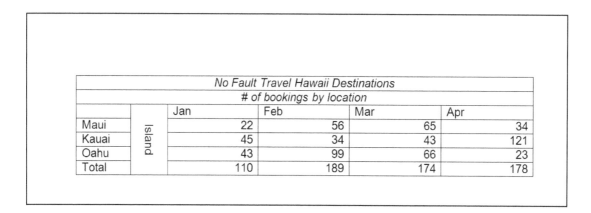

No Fault Travel Hawaii Destinations					
# of bookings by location					
		Jan	Feb	Mar	Apr
Maui	Island	22	56	65	34
Kauai		45	34	43	121
Oahu		43	99	66	23
Total		110	189	174	178

5.   Repeat this process for the remaining totals.

You should now see computed totals for every month.

6.   Select the cells with the month names and then click the Center tool on the Home tab.

Not to confuse you, but if you had use the keyboard shortcut command of (Control+E), you would have saved a step.

Using the Table Styles

Word provides many preformatted Table styles to choose from. You can always manually change the borders and shading if you like, but using a preformatted style can be much faster.

1.   **Ensure that the insertion point is somewhere in this table. Then, display the Design tab and click the More down arrow in the Table styles section.**

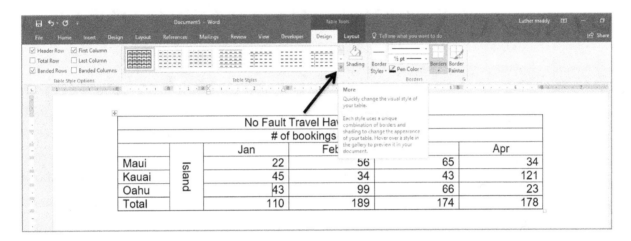

2.   **From the list of Table Styles, scroll down to and select Grid Table 5 Dark Accent 2.**

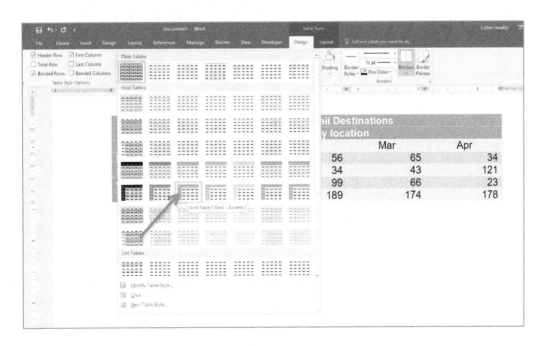

The exact table style you apply here will not matter that much. Go ahead and experiment if you like. If you apply a table style and later change your mind, you can apply any other style from this list. When you do, the existing style is completely erased and the new style takes over.

Changing Column Widths

If you examine this table closely you may notice that the columns do not need to be as wide as they are. In fact, making the width of the columns with the numbers smaller would probably enhance the appearance of this table. There are, of course, several ways to change the width of a column within a table, but for this exercise we'll have you use the Auto Fit method.

3.   **In the Layout tab click the Autofit tool and choose AutoFit Contents.**

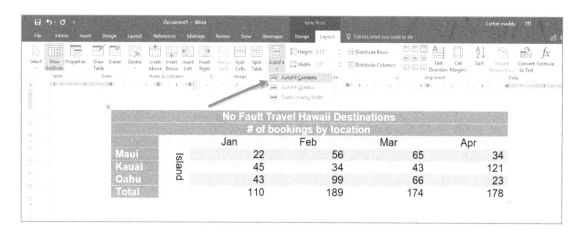

You should notice that the table is much smaller as Word adjusted each column to fit the width of the text within it.

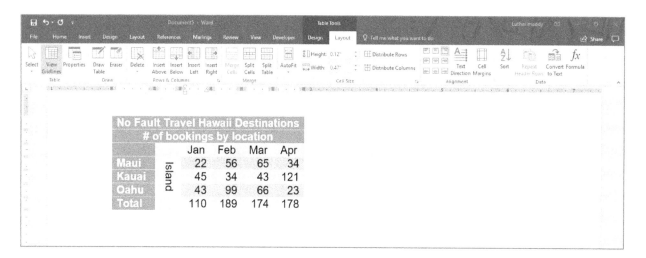

Now you'll center the table on the page by using the Table Properties dialog box.

7. Right-click in the table and choose Table Properties from the shortcut menu.

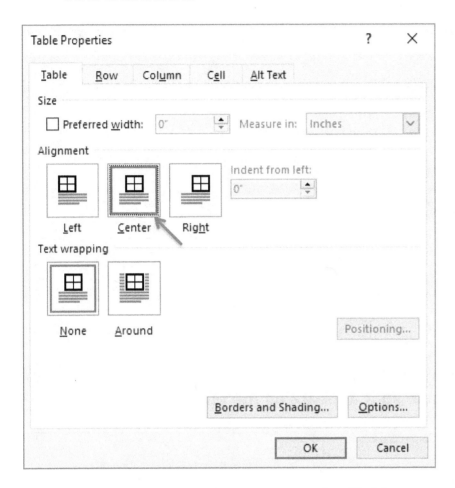

8. Click the Table tab to ensure the Table properties are showing then click the Center tool in the Alignment Section.

You are telling Word that you want the table to be in the center of the page rather than aligned with the left margin.

9. Click OK when done.

The table should be horizontally centered on the page.

10. Save this as *Hawaii Destinations* and close it.

Skill Builder: Lesson #7

1.   Open *Airfare Request.*

2.   Delete the list of airlines and prices and replace it with a table as shown.

No Fault Travel Agency

143 San Andreas Fault Line
Hollister, CA 93992

As requested, we are enclosing a list of the current airfares from Boise to Maui. Please be advised that these fares are subject to change at any moment. Let us know as soon as possible when you're ready to book one of these flights.

Airline	One way fare
Southwest	225.00
United	444.00
Delta	1019.00
Alaska	89.99

Sincerely,

3.   Use the table properties dialog box to change the column widths and center the table so it appears as the one below:

As requested, we are enclosing a list of the current airfares from Boise to Maui. Please be advised that these fares are subject to change at any moment. Let us know as soon as possible when you're ready to book one of these flights.

Airline	One way fare
Southwest	225.00
United	444.00
Delta	1019.00
Alaska	89.99

Sincerely,

4.   Apply an attractive table formatting style and then Save and Close this file.

© 2017 Luther M. Maddy III

Microsoft Word Shortcut Keys

Feature	Shortcut key
Align Center	(Control + E)
Align Justify	(Control + J)
Align Left	(Control + L)
Align Right	(Control + R)
Close a file	(Control + W)
Copy text or graphics	(Control + C)
Cut selected text to the clipboard	(Control +X)
Font	(Control +D)
Increase Indent	(Control + M)
Italic	(Control + I)
Margin Release (hanging indent)	(Control + T)
Page Break	(Control + Enter)
Paste the clipboard contents	(Control + V)
Print	(Control + P)
Redo	(Control + Y)
Replace	(Control + H)
Save	(Control + S)
Underline	(Control + U)
Undo	(Control + Z)

Index

Other books that may interest you

Excel: The Basics (2016, 2013 or 2010)
In "learning by doing" you will gain a good grasp of the basics of Excel. You'll learn to create formulas, format and print worksheets, copy and move cell data, and generate attractive charts and graphs from your Excel data.

Retail price: $10.95

Access: The Basics (2016, 2013)
In this course Access users will learn to: Understand Basic Database Design Techniques Create, Modify and Use Tables Create, Modify and Use Forms Create, Modify and Use Reports and Mailing Labels Create Database Relationships Enter, Edit, and Find Records Create, Edit and Use Queries Use Field Properties and Validation Rules Add Drop-down Lists to Forms
Retail price: $12.95

Excel: Database and Statistical Features (2016, 2013 or 2010)
In "learning by doing" you will gain a good grasp of the Excel database features. You'll learn to create and use Pivot Tables and Charts. You'll also learn about database functions like DSum() and DAverage(). You'll also learn about filtering and subtotaling Excel data. Finally, you'll learn about performing statistical analysis using the Analysis Toolpak.

Retail price: $9.95

Word: The Basics (2013 or 2010)
In "learning by doing" you will learn the basics of MS Word. You'll also be introduced to performing tasks the most efficient way possible to increase your productivity. This workbook covers document creation and editing. You'll learn to copy and move and enhance text. You'll also learn about page a paragraph formatting, setting tabs, creating tables and more.

2013: Retail price: $9.95   2010: Retail price: $8.95

Word: Enhancing Documents (2013 or 2010)
In "learning by doing" you will learn the some of the desktop publishing features of Word. You'll learn to place text in columns, use Autoshapes, enhance mailing labels, and use and create styles. You'll also learn to add hyperlinks to your documents, how to use pre-defined templates, and much more.

2013: Retail price: $9.95   2010: Retail price: $8.95

PowerPoint: The Basics (2016, 2013 or 2010)
In this "learning by doing" course you will learn to: Create and run presentations, Apply and modify design themes, Insert clipart, audio, and video clips, Apply and use slide transitions, Print audience handouts and speaker notes and much more

Retail price: $9.95

Order wherever books are sold. Ordering in quantity?
Save up to 20% by ordering on our website: **www.Pro-aut.com**